C| 2 3 APR 2004

7 – DAY LOAN

M   ...ICES

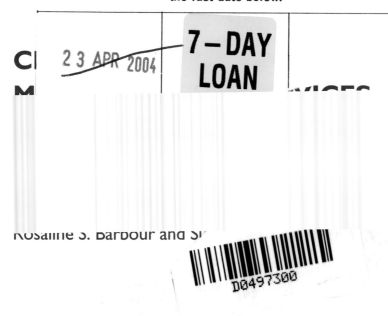

Rosaline S. Barbour and S...

D0497300

The POLICY
P≈P
P R E S S

First published in Great Britain in September 2003 by

The Policy Press
University of Bristol
Fourth Floor, Beacon House
Queen's Road
Bristol BS8 1QU
UK

Tel +44 (0)117 331 4054
Fax +44 (0)117 331 4093
e-mail tpp-info@bristol.ac.uk
www.policypress.org.uk

British Library Cataloguing in Publication Data

A catalogue record for this book is available from the British Library

ISBN 1 86134 427 9 paperback

Nicky Stanley is a Senior Lecturer in Social Work and **Bridget Penhale** is a Lecturer in Social Work, both at the University of Hull. **Denise Riordan** is a Child and Adolescent Psychiatrist based at the Fleming Nuffield Unit, Newcastle upon Tyne. **Rosaline S. Barbour** is Chair of Health and Social Care at the University of Dundee. **Sue Holden** is a Research Associate at the Institute of Learning, University of Hull.

The right of Nicky Stanley, Bridget Penhale, Denise Riordan, Rosaline S. Barbour and Sue Holden to be identified as authors of this work has been asserted by them in accordance with the 1988 Copyright, Designs and Patents Act.

Cover design by Qube Design Associates, Bristol
Front cover: photograph supplied by www.JohnBirdsall.co.uk
Printed and bound in Great Britain by Bell & Bain Ltd, Glasgow

Contents

List of tables and figures

Tables

Figure

Introduction

In the context of family life, children are usually portrayed as dependent and as more vulnerable than their parents; their needs are accorded some priority in recognition of their rights to protection. When parents themselves are vulnerable, agencies' standard responses to families are called into question.

This book is concerned with the professional response to families where mothers have mental health problems and there are concerns about the children's

professionals with a remit to work with all family members; the majority of health professionals work with either children or adults. In social care, practitioners also have a primary focus on either children or adults, and agency structures reinforce this divide. Although a range of national and local developments have aimed to promote interprofessional and interagency work between health and social care services, such shifts have been located *within* adult services or *within* services for children. Increasingly, adult mental health services are provided by joint trusts or teams in which the work of social services and community health staff is integrated. In child care, the emergence of Children's Trusts (DWP, 2002) signals a shift towards similar models for the delivery of a range of health and social care services. The gulf between children's and adults' services remains difficult to bridge. While both mental health and child care practitioners may acknowledge and recognise the contribution of other family members to the welfare and health of their primary client group, service structures will render those providing services to other family members more distant and less accessible. Professional identities and allegiances may act to reinforce structural divisions.

A focus on mothers' mental health requires some explanation. Despite their increasing participation in the workforce, mothers have retained their primary responsibility for child care (Ferri and Smith, 1996). They are also the carers who have the highest levels of contact with a range of health and welfare services (Williams et al, 1986) and are most likely to have their parenting scrutinised by statutory services (Farmer and Owen, 1995; O'Hagan and Dillenburger, 1995). While there is increasing government and research interest in the role played by fathers in families, their contribution to child development (Ryan, 2000) and the extent to which services are responsive to fathers' needs

(Ghate et al, 2000; Daniel and Taylor, 2001), mothers are still positioned in both lay and professional discourses as the key determinants of children's welfare. One of the main themes of this book is the difficulty of constructing a service response that maintains a focus on the needs of both mothers and their children.

Mothers with mental health problems are likely to be lone parents (Targosz et al, 2003), and service responses need to acknowledge the possibility of an absence of emotional and practical support on a day-to-day basis. Lone parenthood confers a range of disadvantages, including low income, isolation, poor housing and difficulties in accessing employment (Crow and Hardey, 1991; Kiernan et al, 1997, Marsh et al, 1997), all of which may contribute to the development of mental health problems. Women experience the stress of lone parenthood more acutely and more frequently. Partners and fathers have not been excluded from this study – their role is discussed in Chapter Six of this book – but mothers are the explicit focus here.

The research study

The study described in this book was preceded by a pilot study (Stanley and Penhale, 1999) which highlighted the difficulties in coordination and communication between the different professional groups involved with families where mothers' mental health problems coincided with child protection concerns. This study identified interprofessional work as a key area for further investigation, together with questions of how health and social care practitioners conceptualised the needs of such families. Users' perceptions and experiences are an essential part of any evaluation of services and professional perspectives need to be balanced against the views of those receiving services. Therefore, the research study was designed to investigate and incorporate the views of mothers with mental health problems. Bringing the two perspectives together in one book allows the voices of service users and practitioners to be developed into a dialogue which addresses the question of what constitutes an effective service response.

Research objectives were established for the study in collaboration with local steering groups which included a range of agency representatives as well as representatives of user organisations. These objectives can be summarised as follows:

- to investigate the views of mothers with severe mental health problems with regard to their own and their family's needs and how these might be most appropriately met;
- to explore health, social services and voluntary sector practitioners' experiences and conceptions of the needs of families where mothers have severe mental health problems and where child protection concerns have been identified;
- to identify the barriers to effective communication and collaboration between practitioners and agencies;

- to establish what resources are valuable for such families from both service users' and professionals' perspectives.

The study, which was carried out between 1999 and 2000 in two research sites, incorporated three main stages.

Stage One

In this phase of the study, a series of interprofessional focus groups was held in 1999 with staff from health, social services and the voluntary sector in an area

Five hundred professionals in health,

two research sites completed a postal questionnaire in 1999. The survey focused on exploring practitioners' attitudes towards families where maternal mental health problems and child care concerns coincided, as well as examining their views on relevant resources for such families and experience of interprofessional work in this area. The findings from this stage of the research are described in Chapters Eight to Eleven.

Stage Three

In the final stage of the research, in-depth interviews with 11 women with severe mental health problems were completed between 1999 and 2000. The first interview used a semi-structured interview schedule that allowed for the collection of detailed information relating to the women's backgrounds and experiences of services. Follow-up interviews were undertaken five to six months later using a less structured approach, which allowed more opportunity to explore perceptions of need, as well as professional and informal support. Chapters Six and Seven report on the mothers' experiences and views.

About this book

The main part of this book is devoted to reporting the findings of the research study. The methodology adopted for this study encompassed both quantitative and qualitative approaches and, in writing the findings up, we have aimed both to convey the statistical findings and allow the women and practitioners to 'speak for themselves'. The first three chapters of the book provide a context for the research study. Chapter One explores the theoretical work and research on mothers' mental health and its impact on children. Chapter Two examines the service configurations of the main agencies delivering services to mothers with mental health needs and their children and discusses recent organisational developments in order to establish the extent to which these services are equipped to respond to the needs of such families. Chapter Three considers the research evidence on interprofessional collaboration and communication, in particular that which relates to work in child protection and mental health services.

In Chapter Four, we outline the methodology used for the research and report on the pilot study completed in 1997. Chapter Five describes the focus groups that informed the design of the two main stages of the research, and Chapters Six to Eleven report the findings of the study. Our concluding chapter, Chapter Twelve, presents the recommendations arising from this project and draws some conclusions in relation to conceptualising mothers' mental health needs. We propose a new model aimed at enhancing the professional responses to these needs.

Throughout this book we utilise a social model of mental health which emphasises the processes through which mental health needs are constructed as well as the social origins of mental health problems. The language used reflects this approach; therefore, medical terminology such as 'psychiatric illness' or 'mental disorder' is avoided, unless we are citing another writer who has used such terms. The terms most commonly employed throughout the book are 'mental health needs' and 'mental health problems'. It is hoped that such language will be accessible to a wide range of professionals and will avoid further stigmatisation of groups that are already heavily stigmatised.

This book identifies the professional and service divides that make it difficult for health and social care practitioners to respond effectively to the interaction of parents' and children's needs. For families, the experiences of parents and children "cannot be compartmentalised" (DoH, 1995a, p 44). Therefore, an effective service response will be one that acknowledges the ways in which the needs of different family members, in some respects and at some times, will overlap, while at other times and in some aspects will be distinct or conflicting. The evidence presented here suggests that, at present, services rarely achieve the flexibility and coordination that such an approach demands. The research aims to pinpoint the ways in which services could be improved and offers some concrete proposals as to how agencies could work together to meet the needs of these families.

We have written this book with a range of professional groups in mind, and we hope that most practitioners involved in this area of work will find something relevant here. Inevitably, our attention has tended to focus on those professional groups that are most heavily engaged with mothers with mental health problems and their children. As an interprofessional team of researchers and practitioners, we have attempted to be even-handed in our account of the interplay between different professional groups. We doubt that we have achieved a viewpoint that is completely objective and untouched by our own professional allegiances and service backgrounds (although some of us have worked in a number of agency settings). Rather than strive for an objective voice that is ultimately both elusive and unattainable, we have chosen instead to convey some of the conflicts and complexities that arise when health and social care professionals are engaged in work with mothers with mental needs and when risks for children come to the fore.

ONE

Mental health needs and mothering

This chapter examines the ways in which the mental health needs of mothers are conceptualised within health and social care. Mothering is simultaneously identified as a prime site of origin for women's mental health problems and a

satisfaction and pride, in the context

research has tended to focus on adverse outcomes. Positive outcomes for parents with mental health problems and their children are rarely noted.

The dual representation of motherhood is supported by a wide range of popular media images of mothers (Coward, 1997). These include the 'harassed mum', the 'dual-career mum', the 'stay-at-home mum', the 'feckless teenage mum', the 'glamorous Victoria Beckham mum' and (an image popularised by Cherie Booth, the wife of the Prime Minister) the 'juggling mum'. The juxtaposition of images and the diversity evident in these representations of motherhood reflect mothers' subjective experience of ambivalence. Featherstone (1997) identifies this ambivalence as a key characteristic of modern mothering and suggests that, in the face of the conflict between the adult's need for autonomy and the child's need for dependence, some feminist theorists have ducked the question of how children's developmental needs are best met. Mental health and child care services have also been slow to identify the significance of this conflict for their clients, and it can be argued that services have made little progress in offering mothers solutions to the dilemmas that arise when their own mental health needs conflict with their children's needs for secure parenting.

The chapter explores the different theoretical models that have been developed to explain women's mental health needs. In particular, research that draws attention to social roles and life events, especially experience of abuse, will be discussed. The evidence for the impact of parental mental health problems on children will be critically examined and this account will be balanced by consideration of the research reporting service users' perspectives. Finally, the chapter addresses the association that has been forged between risk and maternal mental health problems.

Conceptualising women's mental health needs

The preponderance of women in the rates for depression and anxiety constitutes a major gender difference in the mental health of the developed world. While women's rates of admission to psychiatric hospital in the UK were substantially higher than men's in the 1970s and 1980s, the gap has since narrowed (Pilgrim and Rogers, 1999). However, women continue to be significantly more likely to be diagnosed with anxiety, depression and eating disorders while men dominate the diagnosis figures for substance misuse and anti-social personality disorders (Gold, 1998). Meltzer et al's (1995) community study found a similar picture and identified markedly higher rates of neurotic disorders in women, a higher prevalence of substance misuse among men and an even balance between the sexes for figures relating to functional psychoses. Prior (1999) argues that international figures show a similar distribution, and she cites Jenkins' (1996) claim that women are twice as likely to become depressed as men, not just in North America and Europe, but rather across a wide range of cultures. Regier et al (1988) identified considerable variation in the overall monthly rates for depressive disorders in different parts of the world, but found women's affective disorders occurring at a rate twice as high as those of men in London, Australia and Athens.

A number of different theories can be evoked to account for women's over-representation in relation to depression and anxiety. Biological accounts of mental health problems in women focus on the impact of the hormonal activity that characterises the menstrual cycle and the menopause on women's mental health (Scott, 2000) as well as investigating the contribution of the physiological processes involved in giving birth. However, most writers and researchers also acknowledge the effects of changes in social roles and relationships in the period surrounding birth (see Kohen, 2000). Awareness of the risks to mothers' mental health in this perinatal period has been heightened following the publication of the report of the Confidential Inquiries into Maternal Deaths in the United Kingdom (2001). This report highlighted suicide as the most frequent cause of maternal deaths and a more likely cause of death than any medical conditions arising directly from pregnancy or birth. This finding has the effect of shifting attention away from an exclusive focus on the needs of the developing foetus and the new baby to consider the mental health needs of mothers at this stage in their lives.

An alternative explanation to biological accounts is provided by a combination of labelling theory and social constructivism, which suggests that the gender distribution of mental disorders is determined by how mental health problems are defined and by whom. Feminist writers such as Chesler (1972) and Showalter (1987) have argued that, under patriarchy, women's behaviour is pathologised and defined as 'other'. The most celebrated study providing evidence of this process at work in the psychiatric profession was undertaken by Broverman et al in 1970. They found that clinicians' definition of healthy behaviour was commensurate with their conceptions of male behaviour, while female behaviour was conceptualised in negative terms. Prior (1999) claims that an awareness of such processes of stereotyping and their impact on diagnosis is increasingly more evident in psychiatric literature. She suggests that the most current form of gender stereotyping in the arena of mental health is the association between male behaviour and dangerousness. However, we shall note later in this chapter how mothers are also vulnerable to an association between mental health problems and risk.

Women are more likely than men to identify themselves as in need of professional help and are considered to be more willing to disclose distress and to define their problems in terms of mental health need (Dohrenwend and

1992).

An alternative account to theories of labelling/social constructivism focuses on women's social roles as an explanation for women's predominance in the figures for depression and anxiety. This theoretical model emphasises the multiplicity of roles assumed by women once they become mothers, the demands of the caring role, which encompasses care for both children and disabled adults, and women's increased exposure to the stresses of poverty and social isolation.

Brown and his colleagues, who have researched depression in working-class women in London over a period of 20 years, have developed the most comprehensive account of the social origins of depression in women. Brown and Harris' (1978) first major study posited that depression in women was produced by the interaction of vulnerability factors, life events or provoking agents and symptom formation factors. Vulnerability factors included the loss of a mother before the age of 11, the absence of a confiding relationship, lack of employment and three or more children in the home. The life events that precipitated a depressive episode could be a loss through bereavement or separation, a chronic difficulty such as illness, or poor housing. Symptom formation factors determined the severity of the depressive episode and included a history of previous depressive episodes and loss of mother at an early age. Chapter Six of this book provides considerable evidence of isolation and bereavement as common experiences for the mothers with severe mental health problems interviewed as part of the study.

Brown and his colleagues have developed their theory through further research (Brown et al, 1990, 1994) that has resulted in a refining of their original models of life events and vulnerability factors. In the light of the research team's later work in Islington, the life events most likely to provoke depression are defined as those that involve humiliation, devaluation of the self and entrapment (Brown, 1996). The model of vulnerability factors has been extended to include low self-esteem and negative environmental factors which can include poor relationships with a partner or child and the lack of a confiding relationship for single mothers (Brown, 1996).

The increased vulnerability of single mothers to depression has been emphasised by Targosz et al's (2003) study of depression in women which used data from the British National Survey of Psychiatric Morbidity. Thirty per cent of lone mothers were identified as having a mental disorder and prevalence rates for depression were found to be more than three times higher among lone mothers than for either women sharing their household with another adult or women without children aged under 16. Lone mothers were less likely to be in employment than mothers living with another adult, and were half as likely as other women to have access to a car. Targosz et al (2003) argue that the relationship between lone motherhood and depression in their data was explained almost totally by economic and social disadvantage.

Women's experience of abuse

Research exploring the long-term effects of abuse in childhood has identified an association between such abuse and mental health problems in adult life (Mullen et al, 1993; Jumper, 1995; Neumann et al, 1996). Girls are more vulnerable to sexual abuse than boys (Finkelhor, 1994; Cawson et al, 2000) and sexual abuse may be experienced as particularly traumatic because of the secrecy, betrayal of trust and stigma which surrounds it. Bifulco and Moran (1998) have brought together data concerning the impact of childhood abuse from the research studies undertaken by Brown and his team in London. They found a high rate of suicide attempts in childhood and the highest rates of depression among those women who had experienced sexual abuse compared with other women in their representative sample. In Chapter Six, we report significant levels of experience of childhood sexual abuse among the women interviewed for this study. Most of these mothers were themselves convinced that their experience of abuse in childhood had contributed to their mental health problems as an adult. Over half the mothers included in Sheppard and Kelly's study of depressed women (Sheppard with Kelly, 2001) similarly described experience of childhood abuse.

Bifulco and Moran (1998) also draw attention to the long-term sequelae of other forms of childhood abuse, including neglect and psychological abuse. They emphasise that the small group of women in their studies with the worst outcomes were those who experienced a combination of different forms of abuse. However, they point out that their finding that one in three women experiencing adversity in childhood became depressed in the year of interview indicates that many women do survive childhood abuse without encountering depression. Their work contains some important findings on resilience: part-time work and educational achievement were found to offer some women an escape route from the effects of abuse. These results constitute important messages for services.

The experience of abuse in childhood can be reproduced in adult life in the form of domestic violence. Bifulco and Moran (1998) identified a relationship between childhood abuse and experience of physical or sexual assault in early adult life. However, domestic violence is a widespread experience for women (Home Office, 1999) and can occur independently of experience of childhood abuse. Reviews of the US literature (Cascardi et al, 1999; Golding, 1999) identify consistently high rates of depression among women who have experienced domestic violence. In addition to the relationship with depression,

children were defined as abused by social workers

abuse or domestic violence in their adult lives. He argues that "these women were living in families pervaded by abuse and violence" (Sheppard, 1997, p 99). Similarly, all 13 mothers with mental health problems involved with child protection services and included in the pilot study for this project (Stanley and Penhale, 1999) were found to have experienced domestic violence in adult life (see Chapter Four of this book for a full discussion).

The role of women's life events, particularly abuse, in contributing to their mental health needs is increasingly more widely acknowledged and the consultative document for a national women's mental health strategy (DoH, 2002a) highlights the significance of abusive experiences in the development of women's mental health problems. Some of the comments on relevant resources made by practitioners responding to the survey reported in Chapter Eleven of this book display an awareness of the importance of various forms of support and therapeutic services for the mental health of mothers who have experienced abuse. Busfield (1996) offers a model of women's mental health needs that combines both labelling theory and the psychosocial model with its focus on life events and how they are interpreted and mediated. She develops a convincing analysis of the ways in which power differentials between the sexes lead women's disruptive behaviour to be regarded as irrational and uncontrolled. However, she also argues that women's powerlessness renders their experiences of loss and trauma particularly harsh:

> Women's relative lack of power in many situations in comparison with men, and the perceptions surrounding their lack of power makes it more likely that their behaviours may be viewed as indicative of mental disorder. And, on the

other hand, it makes certain experiences more traumatic or distressing. (Busfield, 1996, p 236)

This integrated approach to conceptualising women's mental health needs is likely to be attractive to practitioners who are often acutely aware of the dangers of labelling women's distress as mental illness (Barbour et al, 2002), while also maintaining a realistic appreciation of the social stresses experienced by mothers. However, it is notable that research and other writings that explore the impact of mothers' mental health problems on their children tend to make little use of labelling or social constructivist theories. The emphasis in such studies, rather, tends to be on psychosocial and biogenetic accounts of mental health need.

The impact of maternal mental health needs on children

Parenting capacity is one of the three domains for assessment identified in current government guidance on assessment of children in need. The *Framework for the assessment of children in need and their families* (DoH et al, 2000) identifies parental mental health problems as a factor which can "adversely affect a parent's ability to respond to the needs of his or her child" (DoH et al, 2000, p 25). The guidance continues:

> While some children grow up apparently unscathed, others exhibit emotional and behavioural disorders as a result of these childhood experiences. (DoH et al, 2000, p 25)

The acknowledgement of the difficulty of predicting outcomes for children living with parents with mental health problems, combined with recognition of children's capacity to survive early adversity, reflects the growing interest in resilience that is also evident in the research reviews undertaken by Falkov (1998) and Cleaver et al (1999). This approach to parental mental health problems, which simultaneously identifies their role in contributing to adverse outcomes for children while emphasising the capacity of children to survive the impact of such problems, derives from the work of Michael Rutter. Rutter's research has provided evidence for the negative effects of parental mental illness on children (Quinton and Rutter, 1985; Rutter, 1990) and he has also done much to promote the concept of resilience (Rutter, 1985).

Quinton and Rutter's (1985) four-year longitudinal study explored the effects of parental psychiatric disorder on children. It found that, while the extent to which children were exposed to parental mental illness was relevant, "parental hostility, irritability, aggression and violence" (1985, p 126) in relationships between the parents and in their relationships with the child were more significant in contributing to high levels of psychiatric risk for the children in the period studied. Personality disorder in the parents was also strongly associated with mental health problems in the children. As Quinton and Rutter note, it is difficult to unpick the relationship between what would now commonly be described as domestic violence (since this term is now generally taken to encompass verbal and emotional abuse as well as physical violence) and mental health problems in parents. They envisage three possible relationships that are reproduced here, substituting the term domestic violence for their phrase of 'marital discord':

- domestic violence contributes to mental health problems;
- mental health problems contribute to hostility and violence between parents;
- both domestic violence and mental health problems are the product of other factors such as childhood adversity or social deprivation. (Adapted

takes Rutter's findings on the effects of maternal mental health problems as the starting point for detailed analysis of the impact of postnatal depression on children's development. Cox et al's (1987) study of mother–child interactions in a sample of 76 urban working-class families found that depressed mothers were less likely than those in the control group to pick up on their children's cues. However, physical contact and affectionate touching were more common in the depressed group of mothers. In common with Brown and Harris (1978), they found that the depressed mothers were more likely to be experiencing a range of adversities, including poor housing, problems in the local environment and marital problems. Problems with neighbours were also associated with depression, indicating perhaps the significance of the immediate surroundings in the restricted world of mothers with pre-school children. Depressed mothers were more likely to have had their first children at an early age. Like Rutter, Brown and Harris (1978) found that the extent to which the child was exposed to hostility was a significant factor in the mental status of the children studied and in their capacity to improve.

Murray et al's (1996) study explored the effects of postnatal depression on children aged five and was conducted in Cambridge using a more affluent and better-educated sample of mothers. This study found no association between postnatal depression and cognitive development at five years, although the quality of mother–infant interactions at two months appeared to impact on cognitive performance at five years.

Given that the evidence indicates that maternal mental health problems alone do not impair children's development, it is hard to understand why research has continued to focus so heavily on mothers' parenting skills. It may be that child–parent interactions that can be captured on five minutes of videotape are easier to study than the effects of domestic violence, poor housing or restrictive and hostile neighbourhoods. The predominance of psychiatric and psychological models of research in this field appear to have had the effect of concentrating attention on the potential for the mental health problems of mothers to impair children's development.

Cleaver et al's (1999) research review on the impact of parental problems on parenting capacity has been influential in the development of the *Framework for the assessment of children in need and their families* (DoH et al, 2000) and the tools that accompany the guidance. Their review explores the effects of parental mental illness, alcohol and drug misuse and domestic violence, and notes that domestic violence can contribute to depression and other negative psychological states. They suggest that "in isolation problem alcohol/drug use or mental illness of a parent presents little risk of significant harm to children" (Cleaver et al, 1999, p 23), and argue that children are most vulnerable when domestic violence *coexists* with drug/alcohol misuse or parental mental health problems. However, the review does not offer an in-depth exploration of the association between mothers' experience of violence and mental health problems, nor does it assess the likelihood of the two coexisting.

Research exploring the effects of mental illness on children is collated and summarised in Falkov's training manual, *Crossing bridges* (1998). While acknowledging that most studies that explore the effects of parental mental illness on children are examining *maternal* mental health problems, the training pack, like Cleaver et al's (1999) review, lacks a focus on gender and does not address the social construction of mental illness. Yet for practitioners, anxieties about 'labelling' service users are not insignificant and loomed large in the focus group stage of the research reported in Chapter Five of this book (for a fuller discussion, see Barbour et al, 2002). Sheppard and Kelly (2001) suggest that social workers' awareness of the extent to which mental health problems are a product of women's deprived and stressful environments may result in a failure to recognise mental health needs and act as a barrier to effective intervention.

Falkov's *Crossing bridges* (1998) summarises the potential impact of mental health problems on parenting and the consequences for children. Inconsistency and lack of predictability are identified as possible effects of all mental health problems, while emotional inaccessibility and unresponsiveness to the child's needs are highlighted as features of both depressive disorders and the 'negative' features of schizophrenia. Parenting that is distinguished by severe and persistent forms of these characteristics might constitute severe neglect. Other possible parenting behaviours explored include role reversal, in which parents seek comfort and support from children and inappropriate expectations for self-care and maturity in a child. Finally, parental over-involvement with the child is identified as a possible consequence of both personality disorder and psychotic disorders. In the case of personality disorder, over-involvement may take the form of harsh discipline or criticism; in the case of schizophrenia, it may entail the children being incorporated into paranoid or threatening delusions. Cassell and Coleman (1995) have also emphasised the risks for children inherent in such situations and this evidence was used to inform the design of the vignettes included in the survey (see Chapter Nine of this book).

The problems in parenting detailed above are described in *Crossing bridges* as contributing to impaired development in a number of arenas for children, including cognitive development, language, attention and concentration span, educational achievement and social, emotional and behavioural development (Falkov, 1998, p 57). Like Cleaver et al (1999), Falkov stresses that these effects will be mediated by a number of factors, such as the child's age, developmental stage and the availability of other caring relationships. The pervasiveness and

potential for conflict between the needs of different family members explicit. Work in this field demonstrates a tension between emphasising the deleterious effects of caring for parents with disabilities, mental health problems or long-term illnesses, and focusing on the rights of such families to appropriate and adequate support services. The research on young carers differs from that on the impact of parental mental health problems in that it has tended to be located in social models of care rather than in clinical or psychiatric literature. Earlier literature on young carers emphasised the negative effects of their responsibilities, including restricted educational opportunities, social isolation and stigma (see Becker, 2000, for a review of this literature). However, Olsen and Wates' (2003) research review charts a shift in the work on young carers which has reframed the issue as one of families' entitlement to support and services. They identify a development in the work of the Young Carers Research Group at Loughborough University that has resulted in clear statements about the links between adverse outcomes for young carers and a lack of family support (Dearden and Becker, 2000).

Service users' perspectives

There have been few studies that have examined the perspectives of parents with mental health problems and, with the exception of the literature on young carers, there is also a dearth of research involving children living in such families (Aldridge and Becker, 2003, break new ground in this field). Those studies that have elicited the views of parents with mental health problems provide a useful perspective on the difficulties experienced in relation to services. Hugman and Phillips (1993) interviewed 24 parents who were users of mental health services. These parents reported that social workers tended to attribute all of their difficulties in parenting to their mental health problems and to focus on the risks to children. The manner in which social workers framed their queries was perceived as:"Are your children *at risk from your parenting* because you have mental health needs?". Hugman and Phillips (1993, p 199) suggest that a more appropriate question would have been: "Are you having *any problems in parenting* arising from your mental health needs?". In the face of such attitudes, those parents interviewed expressed an unwillingness to use services. Green and Hyde's (1997) research with families where parents had mental health problems found that families described professional support as intensive and interprofessional during periods of crisis but had limited experience of follow-up work, and received little in the way of preventive work. Families were likely to have either too many or too few professionals involved.

Sands' (1995) US study of 10 lone mothers with severe mental health problems who were participating in a community residential programme compared their views to those of low-income lone mothers who were using a daycare service but did not have mental health problems. She found that the mothers with mental health problems were less likely to voice difficulties and to express a wish for more support, although their needs were considerable. They saw their mental health problems as a continuation of other problems they had experienced, including adverse family circumstances, being looked after and bereavement. Overwhelming, they "wanted to live a normal life" (Sands, 1995, p 94) and, like the control group, saw the experience of mothering as central to their lives.

Sheppard and Kelly's (2001) study of depressed mothers' involvement with child care social work explored women's views of social work intervention. These mothers found the authority wielded by child care social workers oppressive. They "expressed a pervasive fear of losing their children" (2001, p 171) and voiced feelings of exclusion, loss of control, entrapment and blame. Such feelings were particularly evident among those mothers whose children were the subjects of child protection investigations. When social work intervention relied on a family support approach rather than the protection model, mothers were more likely to see child care social workers as friends and to value the emotional support they provided. Chapter Seven of this book describes how the mothers interviewed for the research placed a similar emphasis on supportive listening or counselling.

Farmer and Owen's (1995) research on child protection case conferences explored both child care social workers' responses to mothers with mental health problems and parents' views of the service they received. They found that child protection social workers attached particular importance to the mental health of the mother (1995, p 139). In 11 of the 120 cases in their total sample, the mental health of the female carer was described as poor, and 10 of these cases resulted in the child or children's names being placed on the child protection register. Concerns about mental health problems in lone mothers also contributed to decisions to remove children from their homes. This study also provides useful evidence concerning parents' responses to child protection investigations. Those interviewed found child care social work intervention to be an alienating, stigmatising and disempowering experience. Similar feelings were conveyed by parents in Cleaver and Freeman's (1995) research.

Farmer and Owen's (1995) study is particularly valuable for its gender perspective, which challenges professionals' failure to differentiate parental roles and responsibilities – an omission that too often characterises child protection literature. The study provides strong evidence for Milner's (1993) argument that men are frequently excluded from child care social workers' interventions in families and are thereby rendered 'invisible'. Farmer and Owen found that mothers were the focus of child care social workers' intervention; fathers or ꞏ ꞏ ꞏ ꞏ ꞏ ꞏ ꞏ ꞏ ꞏ ꞏ ꞏ ꞏ ꞏ ꞏ by social workers. Mothers were held

Risk and danger

The *Child protection: Messages from research* (DoH, 1995a) studies were commissioned in the wake of the Cleveland Inquiry to provide a picture of the workings and effectiveness of the child protection system. A number of these studies used substantial case samples to examine families' experiences of child protection intervention and they provide a picture of the extent to which parents with mental health problems figured in the system. Gibbons et al's (1995) research covered the children on child protection registers in eight local authorities. They found that 13% of the children studied were living in a family where a parent or parent figure had been treated for mental illness. In Thoburn et al's (1995) study, nearly 20% of the 220 child protection cases in the sample involved a parent with a mental health problem. While these figures are based on social work records rather than first-hand information or diagnosis, they give some picture of the extent to which parents with mental health problems are involved with the child protection system. Involvement with the child protection system is not necessarily commensurate with children's experience of significant harm. The increased vulnerability of such parents and their contact with services in relation to their mental health needs may render them particularly susceptible to the scrutiny of statutory services and their children may be more likely than those in other families to be judged as at risk of significant harm.

Glaser and Prior's (1997) study of 94 children in four local authorities included on the child protection register under the category of 'emotional abuse' found that parental attributes were the key feature characterising such cases. Parental mental health problems (including suicide attempts/threats) were found in

31% of the families studied. The authors argue that parental mental health problems should be considered as a risk factor for emotional abuse.

Reviews of child deaths have played their part in forging an association between parental mental health needs and high levels of risk for children. James' (1994) study of Part 8 Reviews (the interagency reviews that occur following the death of a child where abuse is confirmed or suspected) found that six of the 30 cases studied involved a parent with mental illness; in five cases this was the mother or stepmother. Falkov (1996) used Part 8 Reviews or records of contact with psychiatric services to identify 32 of the 100 cases included in his study as furnishing evidence of parental psychiatric disorder. This included 25 perpetrators and 10 partners of perpetrators (27 out of the 32 were women). The inclusion of drug dependence as a primary diagnosis in this review might be questioned by those working with a social model of mental health since addiction problems tend to be seen as distinct from mental health problems within this approach. However, even when drug dependence is included in the figures, it needs to be acknowledged that 75% of the perpetrators in the cases reviewed in this influential study did not appear to be suffering from severe mental health problems.

Wilczynski's (1997) study of 48 homicides committed by a parent covered all cases in England and Wales referred by the police to the Director of Public Prosecutions in 1984. In the 48 cases in her sample, just under half the parents had received psychiatric treatment prior to the offence, with a slightly higher proportion being women. Reder and Duncan's (1999) analysis of 49 Part 8 Reviews found that 28 of the caretakers had either a previous history of significant mental health problems or a current disorder at the time of the children's deaths. Reder and Duncan, while noting an association between parental mental health problems and increased risk of child maltreatment, are cautious in their conclusions, emphasising that substance abuse is the parental problem most strongly associated with fatal child abuse. Their analysis found that professionals involved with these families appeared to experience "assessment paralysis" (1999, p 56), which usually focused on the issue of whether the parent concerned had a diagnosable psychiatric disorder among professionals. Ambivalence concerning diagnosis was identified as a common attitude in the focus groups undertaken prior to the study and described in Chapter Five of this book (see Barbour et al, 2002).

Stroud and Pritchard's (2001) analysis of child deaths suggests that violent male child sex abusers represent a much greater danger to children than mothers with severe mental health problems. They emphasise that violence, rather than mental illness, is the main predictor of child deaths. However, the association between parental mental illness and child deaths endures. As Paul Curran, assistant director of Lewisham Social Services, has commented, professionals "outside the specialist Mental Health Services are not immune to the media portrayal of people with mental health problems as 'mad, bad and dangerous'" (Michael Sieff Foundation, 1997, pp 14-15). While an association between mothers' mental health problems and risks for children is undeniable, the strength and nature of that relationship remains vague and ill defined. The research evidence stresses the role of other factors that mediate between mental health problems in parents and harm and danger for children. However, despite being unspecified, the fears evoked by such risks may be sufficient to render health and social care services unsympathetic and threatening in the eyes of mothers. The following chapter identifies the nexus of services that mothers with mental health problems might use and begins with a consideration of the role of risk in shaping those services.

TWO

The service context

In the UK, mental health services for adults and child care social work both owe much of their current structures to a preoccupation with risk. Mental health services are principally concerned with the risks that their user group

context of health and social care, risk tends to be defined negatively and its outcomes are conceptualised as harm or danger (Alaszewski, 2002). A social policy analysis traces the centrality of risk in both child care social work and mental health services to the influence of a series of public inquiries during the last two decades of the 20th century (Stanley and Manthorpe, 2004). At the time of writing, the capacity of inquiries to shape services is apparent in the anticipated organisational changes in child care services that have been stimulated by the inquiry into the death of Victoria Climbié (Laming, 2003). The extent to which inquiries and the public response to them have driven policy is analysed in depth elsewhere (Parton, 1985; Parton, 1991; McCulloch and Parker, 2004: forthcoming; Munro, 2004: forthcoming). However, the influence of the inquiries has had to contend with other imperatives, including concerns about the intrusion of the state into the private sphere and an emphasis on the community or family as the locus of care for vulnerable individuals.

These policy thrusts received their most coherent expression at the same point in time for the two services. While the shift to community care in mental health services was well underway with the closure of many of the large hospitals already completed by 1989 (Barham, 1992), the White Paper – *Caring for people: Community care in the next decade and beyond* (DoH, 1989a) – articulated the new ideology of community care for vulnerable people and instigated the reorganisation of social work services for adults that took place in the 1990s. This reorganisation introduced a purchaser–provider split into adult social work services, and firmly established a divide between this structure and child care social work. The 1989 Children Act simultaneously emphasised the role of the state in keeping families together and heralded a shift away from protection towards prevention that continued and gathered momentum throughout the 1990s.

The ongoing struggle between risk and normalisation has taken different forms as it has been worked out in the two services. Current positions of accommodation or balance are fragile and look to be easily destabilised by the government response to events such as the Victoria Climbié's death or homicides committed by those with mental health problems. This chapter outlines the policy and service context in which mental health professionals and child care workers deliver services, and considers how these structures impact on families where mothers have mental health problems. In addition to considering the context in which adult mental health services and child care social work are delivered, the structures and roles of both primary care and child and adolescent mental health services are also considered. Each of these organisations has been identified as offering a possible key to resolving the problems of delivering services simultaneously to both children and their parents (DoH et al, 1999; Reder and Duncan, 1999), and each is included in this research. Finally, this chapter examines the role of voluntary organisations in providing services for mothers with mental health needs as this sector has been the source of some innovative projects.

Mental health services

Mental health problems cover a broad spectrum, ranging from psychotic illnesses (including schizophrenia) at one extreme to reactive states of depression at the other. When broad definitions of mental health need are employed, epidemiological studies show that between one fifth and one quarter of the general population in Western countries will experience mental health problems at a given point in time (Jenkins et al, 2002). Meltzer et al's (1995) UK survey of mental health problems in adults found that one in six adults had experienced some form of mental health problem in the week prior to interview. The widespread nature of mental health problems coincides with a limited resource base that varies in its size and comprehensiveness across the UK. The initial development of community mental health services in the wake of psychiatric hospital closures was slow and piecemeal: under the Thatcher government, community care was conceived of primarily as care by the family, supplemented only by input from the state when absolutely necessary. The number of in-patient psychiatric beds was drastically reduced in some parts of the country (Powell et al, 1995). Such service shortfalls have resulted in policies that target mental health services on the groups with the highest need. However, measuring levels of need in relation to mental distress can prove difficult. In practice, mental health professionals might find it difficult to compare the needs of a mother of small children who is experiencing acute anxiety symptoms with those of a single person with a long-term schizophrenic illness. Risk has proved a less elusive principal of allocating services than need, and Kemshall

(2002) argues that risk has replaced community care as the key ideology informing mental health services.

The mechanism for determining eligibility for mental health services is the Care Programme Approach (CPA), introduced in 1991. (It is worth noting that the impetus for the CPA was the death of Isabel Schwarz, a social worker at Bexley Hospital who was killed by a service user.) The CPA provides a structure of assessment, review and key working for those users of mental health services with severe and enduring needs. Implementation of the CPA was initially slow and patchy (SSI, 1999), and the various levels of eligibility were determined at a local rather than central level. This resulted in some

'eligibility' for services.

They constituted a response to the long series of inquiries into homicides committed by individuals who had been in contact with mental health services. The Clunis Report (Ritchie et al, 1994) is the best known of these, but in fact 140 mental health inquiry reports were published between 1985 and 2002 (Sheppard, 2004: forthcoming).

The CPA has the effect of targeting services on those assessed as having 'severe and enduring' needs or 'high risk'. In 1999, the CPA was simplified and given a national structure (DoH, 1999a) which should contribute to a more equitable picture in terms of access to services across the country. There are currently two levels at which the CPA can be delivered: 'simple' and 'enhanced'. Service users on the 'enhanced' level of the programme are those who are judged to be either high risk or are receiving complex packages of services. In a reflection of the increasing integration of health-provided mental health services and mental health social work services, the CPA has been integrated with the community care assessment tools used by local authority care managers.

Increasingly, the lack of a preventive arm to mental health services has been acknowledged by government, and there have been some new initiatives aimed at reaching 'hard to reach' groups and those who are in both the early and crisis stages of mental disorder. These interventions include a range of assertive outreach services, early interventions in psychosis and crisis teams (DoH, 2000a). The *National service framework for mental health* (DoH, 1999b) announced some of these initiatives and also boosted the preventive role of GPs by introducing a plan for training psychology graduates to deliver short-term interventions in primary care settings.

While the CPA remains the mechanism for determining priority, the level and configuration of mental health resources in a region is the responsibility of local community health trusts or, increasingly, mental health trusts, which provide and manage both in-patient and community mental health services. Since the early days of hospital almoners, social work has always had a strong foothold within mental health services. The 1983 Mental Health Act formalised that role by developing and strengthening the powers of approved social workers (formerly mental health officers), who were given responsibility for administering and managing formal admissions to hospital. In addition to employing mental health social workers, social services departments have delivered a range of community mental health resources, often from community mental health teams, which are interprofessional and are increasingly run jointly with health services. In line with the government's insistence on health and social care organisations planning and delivering joint services (DoH, 1998a), it is becoming common for all community mental health services within a locality to be managed and delivered by health and social services departments working in partnership.

In addition to specifying the type of services that local trusts should be seeking to develop and commission, the *National service framework for mental health* (DoH, 1999b) emphasises the need to develop the quality of the service and to involve mental health users and their families more actively in the planning and delivery of services. The framework acknowledges the necessity for further training of staff who are working in mental health services. It also stresses the importance of services being accessible to those who wish to use them. The roots of this approach lie in the increasing recognition that services have to earn compliance from their users rather than demanding it. In the *Report of the confidential inquiry into homicides and suicides by mentally ill people*, Boyd (1996) argued that the quality of the service was a significant factor in persuading people to engage with its staff:

> It must be asked whether the service being offered some patients – crowded wards, unsuitable fellow patients, overworked staff – may not play an important part in leading them to distance themselves from treatment they need. (Boyd, 1996, p 60)

However, emphasis on the quality of the service and a new interest in consultation with service users and their families have not replaced a focus on risk. The enduring nature of this theme is evident in the draft Mental Health Bill (DoH, 2002b), where risk, its level and whether or not it involves the patient or others are all identified as key components of the definition of mental disorder. Critics of the bill have argued that its effects are likely to work against the vision of accessible user-friendly services promoted by the *National service framework for mental health* (DoH, 1996).

What are the implications for mothers who need and use mental health services? Despite the increasing emphasis on preventive approaches in mental health services, these approaches do tend to be limited in their scope. Services are still primarily focused on those who can be classified as having 'severe and enduring' needs or those who pose a risk to others. As noted in Chapter One of this book, women are more likely to be diagnosed with the milder forms of depression and neurotic disorders which can be conceptualised as explicable responses to personal and social experience. Such diagnoses will place them outside the 'severe and enduring' group. For mothers, the quickest route to mental health services is perhaps being identified as a 'high risk', a label which is acquired when they are assessed as representing a risk to their children. Here, the preoccupation with the risk that service users pose to others coincides with the emphasis on the risks to children, which informs work in child protection.

inquiries identified a ....

(London Borough of Brent, 1985) and criticised social workers' focus on the needs of the adults in each family rather than those of the children. The cumulative effect of these inquiries was to move the direction of child and family social work away from the preventive, community-focused approach that had been advocated by the Barclay Report in the early 1980s (Barclay, 1982) towards an emphasis on protection and risk. This shift produced a steep rise in the numbers of children on child protection registers – a rise that continued into the 1990s (Corby, 2000) despite the implementation in 1991 of the 1989 Children Act.

The 1989 Children Act itself was also in part a response to an inquiry – the Cleveland Inquiry (Butler-Sloss, 1988) – although much of the policy direction of the act had already been established by the earlier Short Report (Social Services Committee, 1984) and the *Review of child care law* (DHSS, 1985). The inquiry reported on the removal from home of over 100 children by social workers and paediatricians who considered that there was evidence to indicate that sexual abuse had taken place. While the inquiry report was not able to deliver any definitive view as to whether the children had or had not been abused (court cases were still pending at the point when the inquiry reported), social workers were criticised for intervening in too precipitate a fashion on the basis of questionable evidence. In this case, the rights of families to protection from state interference were judged to have been transgressed. The events in Cleveland made the argument for the relationship between families and child care professionals to be based on partnership rather than antagonism. Partnership with families became a key theme for child care social work in the 1990s: while not explicitly mentioned in the 1989 Children Act, it was emphasised in the accompanying guidance (Home Office et al, 1991; DHSS Inspectorate, 1995).

Cleveland, like the preceding inquiries, also highlighted failures of interprofessional communication and coordination. Therefore, partnership between professionals has been another key theme of child protection work in the wake of these major inquiries. A new version of the *Working together* guidelines was produced in 1991 to replace the 1988 version, and Lupton et al (2001) note that the subtitle of the third version, published in 1999 (DoH et al), substituted the term 'interagency work' for the earlier 'interagency cooperation', implying a fuller integration of the work of different services. At a local level, Area Child Protection Committees (ACPCs) are the organisations currently charged with the task of coordinating the work of the various agencies contributing to the protection of children in any one area. These include child care social workers, health visitors, GPs, paediatricians, relevant hospital staff, particularly those in accident and emergency teams, staff working in voluntary agencies, probation officers, police officers working in child protection or family units, teachers and school nurses. ACPCs are made up of senior representatives from all agencies involved in child protection work in a local authority. They are responsible for developing local guidance and protocol and for delivering relevant training to the range of local professionals involved in child protection. From 1991, they were charged with conducting the Part 8 Reviews into child deaths in their area. Largely, these interagency reviews replaced the formal public inquiry into child deaths which so characterised the 1980s. They have now been redesignated as 'serious case reviews', following the publication of the 1999 edition of the 'Working Together' guidelines (DoH et al, 1999).

The 1989 Children Act reaffirmed the rights of families to bring up their children free from state intervention in a statement of commitment to preserving family life:

> The Act rests on the belief that children are generally best looked after within the family with both parents playing a full part and without resort to legal proceedings. (DoH, 1989b, section 1.3)

This commitment was embodied in Part Three of the Act, which gave local authorities powers to provide preventive services to children and families to support children defined as 'in need'. On the child protection side, the measures for intervening and removing children from their homes were redefined: the Place of Safety Order, which had been heavily used in the events in Cleveland, disappeared. Critics have described the act as attempting to achieve a "balance" or "accommodation" (Fox Harding, 1997, p 186) between the rights of parents and the authority of the state to intervene in family life. Parton (2002) argues that, despite the Act's emphasis on preventive work with families, a preoccupation with the assessment of high risk is discernible in the concept of 'significant harm', which was introduced as the key criterion for triggering the machinery of child protection. As Parton (2002) notes, significant harm does not need to be present; it is enough for it to be "likely" (Children Act 1989, section 31.2). 'Likelihood' requires professionals to predict future harm or, in other words, to assess risk.

The research studies commissioned by the Department of Health in response to the events in Cleveland were summarised in the *Child protection: Messages from research* report (DoH, 1995a). Together with the Audit Commission report, *Seen but not heard* (1994), the findings of the various studies undertaken into the workings of the child protection system in the late 1980s and early 1990s suggested that the system continued to emphasise protection and the assessment of risk at the expense of developing preventive services that supported families

Except in very extreme cases, the needs of parents and children cannot be compartmentalised. (DoH, 1995a, p 44)

However, child protection work was not to be neglected but, rather, was to be viewed as part of the same continuum as services delivered to support families. Family support and child protection were henceforth to be seen as "two sides of the same coin" (DoH et al, 2000, p 5).

Following the publication of *Messages from research* in 1995, local authorities began to refocus their services to develop family support services. Whether or not local authorities have the capacity to achieve this refocusing in the context of a system that is still dominated by risk and child protection work has been questioned (Tunstill, 1997). However, local authority family support services have been augmented by a raft of initiatives funded by central government, which, although patchy in their distribution, have been targeted on localities with high levels of social exclusion. These include Sure Start, which delivers health, childcare and early education services to families with pre-school children; a range of programmes financed through the Children's Fund, which aims to develop preventive services for five- to 13-year-olds; and Connexions, which provides personal support through mentors for socially excluded young people between the ages of 13 and 19. These initiatives are delivered through interagency partnerships and bring together a range of professionals, including midwives, health visitors, nursery nurses, youth workers and careers officers. However, at the time the research described in this book was undertaken, these new area-based initiatives were not yet fully developed and family support services were confined to those provided by local authorities and some of the major voluntary organisations.

The refocusing of child care social work was underpinned by the *Quality protects: Framework for action* programme (DoH, 1998b), which established a range of targets for local authority social services departments. These were aimed both at improving standards of care for children who were 'looked after' and at reducing the numbers of children entering the looked after system. The programme emphasised the need for all children and their families referred to local authority social services departments to undergo a standard assessment procedure. The recommended model was outlined in the new *Framework of assessment for children and their families* (DoH et al, 2000). Following a time-limited initial assessment, children in need now receive an in-depth core assessment which has to be completed within 35 working days. This model was not in place at the time of the study. However, it is worth noting the implications of this new approach to assessment, which, with its emphasis on procedure and form filling, continues the care management approach to child protection work established in the 1990s. This model emphasises assessment and service brokerage rather than therapeutic engagement with service users (Sheppard, 1995).

The model promoted by the new *Framework for assessment* is an ecological approach to assessment which is depicted as a triangle. The three sides represent, in turn, the child's developmental needs, the environment and parenting capacity. Detailed consideration of parental capacity includes exploration of parental mental health as well as consideration of key issues such as substance misuse and domestic violence. The framework also advocates openness with parents regarding causes for concern, stresses the importance of exploring families' strengths as well as their needs, and recommends that a range of professionals should contribute to the assessment process. Early evaluations of the implementation of the *Framework for assessment* have been mixed, with some positive feedback from families (Corby et al, 2002) being balanced by concerns about the dangers of assessment becoming 'form-led' (Horwath, 2002), and the unwieldy and potentially static nature of the ecological model when applied to practice (Sidebotham, 2001). However, the concept of parental capacity provides a useful vehicle for incorporating parents' mental health problems into the process of assessment and is likely to ensure that this aspect of families' needs receives more recognition than was previously the case.

The death of Victoria Climbié has reignited the protection-versus-prevention debate. At the time of writing, the emergence of multi-agency children's trusts (DWP, 2002) has been announced and the publication of the *National service framework for children* is imminent. The structures for the delivery of child care social work look set to change. Such changes may have the effect of making assessment of children and families more truly interprofessional. Children's trusts may also offer a means of continuing to deliver protection and prevention in child care as part of the same service. However, children's and adults' services are likely to move even further apart as they become incorporated iᵣ interagency trusts.

Child and adolescent mental health services

Child and adolescent mental health services (CAMHS) occupy the hinterland between adult mental health services and child health. As a specialist service that is predominantly delivered in the community, it is necessarily closely allied with primary care, as well as with agencies that deliver social care. Working across a wide variety of interfaces, where boundaries between one agency and another can easily become blurred, demands that those within the service are

delivery. While some services were well resourced and adequately statted, this was (and continues to be) the exception rather than the rule. At a time when prevalence rates of mental disorder in the child and adolescent population were of the order of 20% (Meltzer et al, 1999), the majority of services were overwhelmed by the sheer volume of referrals made to them. For many teams, the standard response was for referrals to be prioritised according to the criteria of the particular service. There were frequently long waiting times for an initial assessment, and in some instances a further wait for therapeutic interventions. Services were focused on the individual family; that is, the child or adolescent referred was the target for attention, and most of those referred to a team were seen. As an understandable response to the volume of work they were facing, most teams tended to be reactive rather than preventive in their approach. They saw children or families being referred to them, but did not actively seek contact with other agencies working with vulnerable children and young people with the intention of identifying those at risk and seeking to work proactively. While some services (usually those allied to large teaching hospitals) did have links with other agencies, such as paediatric wards or residential units, these tended to be patchy and to vary according to individual interest rather than as a response to a specifically identified service need.

A significant landmark for CAMHS was the Health Advisory Service report, *Together we stand* (1995). It attempted to bring together the varying and, at times, seemingly competing services working with children and young people with mental health problems and their families. It delineated the varying components of a modern mental health service for children and young people and described the relationships between the professionals that deliver the service. Taking a four-tier approach, it outlined a hierarchical service that had as its foundation comprehensive primary care services, and moved up through different levels of service which aimed to meet different levels of need. In particular, it highlighted the importance of consultation and liaison as an integral part of CAMHS work. It argued that children and young people did not all need to be seen by CAMHS professionals, but that CAMHS professionals needed to acknowledge the training of colleagues in other disciplines and view consultation and liaison with other services as a core component of their responsibilities. However, the subsequent Audit Commission report, *Children in mind* (1999), found that, in the NHS trusts audited, CAMHS professionals spent only 2% of their time providing consultation to others. This report recommended better liaison with other services, particularly the non-specialist services at tier one, such as GPs, health visitors, teachers and school nurses.

During the period that the research described in this book was being conducted, many local services were striving to adopt the model described in *Together we stand*. The danger inherent in this report was that it risked creating the impression that there was a far greater workforce providing mental health services to children and young people than was in reality the case. Professionals such as school nurses, health visitors, residential social workers and teachers might in theory be well placed to deliver primary care level mental health interventions. However, even in the presence of adequate training and supervision, they often lacked the time to do so due to other professional and statutory demands made of them. In addition, *Together we stand* (Health Advisory Service, 1995) described a tiered, hierarchical model which oversimplified the complex, more matrix-like framework within which CAMHS teams actually functioned. The four-tier structure can be criticised as deceptive, both in its scope and in the extent to which it presented the work of different agencies as articulated.

The Mental Health Foundation's *Bright futures* report (1999) identified shortfalls in service provision and stressed the need for earlier preventive interventions in the field of children and young people's mental health. The report argued for both government and local initiatives to be cross-departmental and emphasised the importance of matching resources to need. The government responded to such calls with the introduction of a new mental health grant worth £6 million a year for three years from 1999 (DoH, 1999c). This was to be paid to social services departments with the requirement that spending was informed by joint strategies for children's mental health services agreed with CAMHS. However, take-up of this funding nationally has been variable (Baylis, 2002), and the development of CAMHS services continues to be uneven. For families, access to CAMHS services may be restricted by a number of factors. For example, the YoungMinds (2002) strategy for adolescents points to the variations in the cut-off point for CAMHS services across the country, while Wilson (2002) has drawn attention to the fact that many CAMHS services receive referrals from GPs only, offering no means of direct access for children and families. Some of these issues look likely to be addressed by the *National service framework for children*, which will emphasise the need for CAMHS to develop comprehensive services (DoH, 2003).

Child and adolescent mental health services have traditionally taken the child or young person as the focus of their work. While CAMHS professionals will recognise that children affect, and are affected by, the mental health of their carers, work with parents has tended to focus on parenting issues, and at times on marital relationships. Where parents have mental health problems, this has traditionally been seen as the remit of adult services, with whom the CAMHS team might have only fleeting contact, usually on a case-by-case basis, and often in response to concerns about risk and child protection. Difficulties in ～～～～～ ～～～～～～～～ ～～～～～～～～ ～～～～～～～ (Maitra and Jolley 2000) and a desire

markets within the NHS was superseded by the emergence of primary care groups (PCGs) in 1997, which were swiftly followed by primary care trusts (PCTs) in 2000. General practitioners have moved from a role that was purely clinical to one which embraces the planning, commissioning and management of a range of patient services. Lupton et al (2001, p 133) note that, for GPs, "time has become the key desired 'resource'".

As the role of the GP has become more diverse and complex, GPs have organised themselves into larger practices, a process which was accelerated by the introduction of PCGs. In larger practices, the traditional concept of the 'family doctor' who is familiar with the medical histories of all the members of a family has become increasingly obsolete: patients now see whichever doctor is available when they book an appointment. Individual patients will only see one GP consistently should they be able to plan their appointments around that GP's schedule; otherwise they and their families will move between a number of GPs and locum staff working in their local practice. General practitioners will have to rely on their colleagues' often brief notes to build a picture both of an individual's treatment over time and a family's ongoing contact with primary care services. This fragmentation is compounded by the fact that teamwork in primary care is relatively undeveloped (Poulton and West, 1999).

This development means that GPs' capacity to offer the consistency of a professional relationship over time, something that appears to be of key importance for users of mental health services, is restricted. Likewise, it is unlikely that one practitioner will have an up-to-date awareness of the needs of all the members of one family, although that information may well be held jointly by members of the primary care team. Jenkins et al's (2002) argument that primary care is well placed to provide mental health service users with continuity of care may no longer be valid for such services in England and Wales. However, their point that primary care, as a universal service, is less stigmatising than specialist mental health services is significant for those who use services.

Primary care is the first point of access to mental health services, and it has been estimated that 90% of those with a diagnosable mental health problem will visit their GP (Goldberg and Huxley, 1992; McCulloch, 2003). However, only about 60% of those reaching the GP's surgery will be diagnosed, with 10% of this group being referred on to specialist mental health services. As McCulloch (2003) notes, not only is it the case that the vast majority of those with a mental health problem are seen in primary care, but most of this group will be treated only in this setting. Concerns about primary care's low diagnosis rates in relation to mental health problems have resulted in calls for more mental health training for GPs (Walters, 2003). *The National Service Framework for Mental Health* (NSF) (DoH, 1999b) allocates a central role to primary care in the treatment of mental health problems: GPs will continue to assess and manage the bulk of mental health needs in the community. They will also still provide the main referral route to specialist mental health services. The NSF identifies a shortfall in skills and knowledge in mental health within primary care. To date, GPs have been too preoccupied with organisational changes to respond to pressures to improve their performance in mental health. The NHS Plan (DoH, 2000a) proposes developing special interest GPs, a new breed of clinician which would include GPs specialising in mental health.

As noted above, the capacity of primary care to manage patients with mental health problems will be augmented by 1,000 new mental health workers trained in the delivery of brief therapy. General practitioners have a long history of employing counsellors or working alongside social workers or community psychiatric nurses (CPNs) attached to primary care settings (Lymbery and Millward, 2000; Manthorpe and Iliffe, 2003). Rogers and Pilgrim (2001, p 151) suggest that counsellors in the primary care setting offer GPs an attractive "quick fix" for patients with psychosocial needs, while both social workers and mental health workers are likely to find that their clients appreciate the lack of stigma attached to the primary care setting. Corney and Strathdee (1996) argue that primary care services are highly accessible for women, but also highlight the need for additional female GPs to be recruited to work in the inner cities. Women with children are likely to find surgeries and primary care centres more welcoming to families than mental health resources; the primary care setting may well be more familiar to mothers, as they will frequently also house antenatal clinics, mother and baby clinics and child health services.

Community nurses, including district nurses and health visitors, are also based in primary care settings, although they are currently employed by community health trusts, which provide services on a contractual basis to PCTs. Health visitors are the professional group most likely to have contact with mothers with mental health problems in the community. Like GPs, the universal nature of their service means that their support and advice can be used with relatively little stigma. Most health visitors have been trained to screen for postnatal depression, using the Edinburgh Post Natal Depression Scale (Cox and Holden, 1994), and are likely to have a well-developed knowledge base in relation to this type of mental health problem.

Health visitors are also the health professionals most heavily involved in child protection work. This is a function of their role in monitoring the health of younger children, but is also attributable to their role as a proxy for GPs in child protection work (Birchall with Hallett, 1995). While government guidelines (DoH et al, 1999) envisage a significant role for GPs in child protection, their

The purchaser–provider split introduced by the NHS and 1990 Community Care Act promoted a culture of 'contracting out' which contributed to the growth of the independent sector throughout the 1990s. This ideological and structural shift was fuelled by the distribution of funding. Deakin (2001) reckoned the most striking example of this to be the allocation of 85% of the transitional funds to providers outside the statutory sector. Also, during the 1990s, housing associations, which had expanded following the gradual transfer of investment and some local authority housing to their control in the late 1980s, began to diversify in response to increased competition (Mullins and Riseborough, 2001). This diversification included a move into the care sector, with more housing associations taking on specialist roles in relation to tenants with mental health needs. Simultaneously, voluntary organisations such as MIND expanded their activities as providers of both day and residential care in order to take advantage of the new markets created by the Conservative government's 'mixed economy of welfare' and local authorities' focus on those with the highest levels of need.

However, the expansion of the contract culture has not been without its costs, and Scott and Russell's (2001) case study research involving 27 voluntary organisations in northern England found that agencies were required to devote resources to developing policies and systems to meet commissioners' demands. Negotiating contracts also represented a considerable drain on limited time and energy. Most significantly, the stability and continuity anticipated from longer-term contracts with local authorities had failed to materialise. By 1997, two fifths of the contracts identified by Scott and Russell's survey were still awarded only for one year. Competitive tendering had priced some smaller organisations out of the market.

The key health–social services partnership in mental health is now supplemented by a range of services provided by the independent sector. These include a range of housing and employment services run by housing associations or voluntary organisations, as well as crisis services, education or training initiatives, drop-ins and social groups. Voluntary services are likely to be 'needs led', responding to the needs of particular groups within one locality, such as services for minority ethnic groups (Keating, 2002), carers' groups or groups for individuals with similar needs such as bereavement or schizophrenia. Users' and survivors' groups have also emerged, and some of these have expanded to develop and manage services (Sayce, 2000).

In the independent sector, services for children and families have tended to be dominated by the well-established major voluntary organisations. Some of the mainstream activities of child care social work departments – for instance, assessment work – may be contracted out to them. These organisations may offer specialist assessment or treatment services, perhaps providing therapeutic work with abused children or residential assessment facilities that allow for parenting to be assessed on a 24-hour basis. The needs-focused approach of the voluntary sector has also resulted in organisations targeted on particular groups, such as young carers, disabled children and their families, black or Asian families and families experiencing particular problems such as domestic violence or sexual abuse.

A limited number of voluntary organisations provide services for women with mental health problems in England and Wales. These include the influential Women's Therapy Centre in North London and a number of day centres which work with women with mental health needs alongside other users. Such services have provided models for the development of women-only mental health services envisaged in the Department of Health's consultation document on women's mental health services (DoH, 2002a). The document suggests that the voluntary sector will continue to play a key role in the envisaged expansion of women-only mental health day services. The New Parent Information Network (NEWPIN) is a voluntary organisation which trains volunteers to provide one-to-one and group support to parents with mental health needs. It is established in a number of major cities in England, but not in either of the areas where the research study was undertaken. However, Home-Start, a voluntary agency that delivers support to parents in the home, was accessible to families in both research sites. The service offers flexibility and the potential to respond to need on an individual or family basis, which makes it particularly useful for families where mothers have mental health problems.

Ease of access and flexibility in delivering services are characteristics of voluntary sector organisations, rendering them especially user-friendly. This may be a key issue for mothers with mental health problems (such as depression) who may lack the motivation and organisation required to approach statutory services, with their bureaucratic procedures and gate-keeping processes. Services provided by the voluntary sector can also offer a less threatening alternative to parents who fear losing their children to child care social workers or being subject to coercive treatment regimes by mental health services. Voluntary services are also likely to be responsive to the needs of minority ethnic women. As Ismail (1996) notes, the voluntary sector has assumed ownership of mental health service provision for specific ethnic groups. However, voluntary sector services are also likely to be patchy and under-funded. The precariousness of their existence under the 'contract culture' may make it hard for organisations to retain staff and provide a service that users find consistent and reliable.

This chapter has looked briefly at recent policy developments and service configurations in relation to those key organisations likely to be involved with families when parental mental health problems and child care concerns collide.

continuity of care that the traditional family doctor offered may no longer be available. Voluntary organisations may be able to offer services that are easier to access and less threatening than those provided by the statutory sector. However, the availability of such services will vary from one area to another, and uncertainties concerning funding may threaten their long-term survival. It seems evident that the complexity of needs in such families will require agencies to work together to construct packages of support and intervention which reflect the multiplicity of needs in these families. Chapter Three considers the effectiveness of interprofessional work with families where mental health needs and child care issues coexist.

THREE

Interprofessional work

Before examining the evidence for the extent to which services succeed in working together, it is useful to consider why interprofessional coordination is generally considered a goal worth pursuing. As Corby (2002) has pointed out, ~~the outcomes for service~~

~~range of...~~

by different agencies; for example, information relating to a new partner's history of mental health problems may only be accessed by a child care social worker through contact with mental health services. Coordination and communication between professionals will also allow families to be monitored more effectively. Should the health visitor share her weekly observations of the child with the social worker who is also visiting once a week, a fuller picture covering a wider range of circumstances and situations can be constructed.

The need for information that is reliable and comprehensive (Sheppard, 1990) becomes particularly acute when risks are perceived to be significant. Guidelines on professional codes of confidentiality recognise this and allow for information to be disclosed to relevant agencies without clients' consent when risks are assessed as high. However, judging whether or not the risks are high enough to warrant breaching professional codes of confidentiality may vary according to individual assessments of the level of risk, the value attached to confidentiality and users' rights by different professional groups, and the client orientation of the practitioner making the decision.

Even when information is available, professionals may experience difficulties in collating, sifting and interpreting it (Sheppard, 1990; Waterhouse and Carnie, 1992; Farmer and Owen, 1995). These tasks, and the decision making which ensues, are likely to involve the assessment of risk, and much of the process is undertaken in multi-professional forums such as child protection case conferences, ward rounds or Care Programme Approach (CPA) reviews. An interprofessional approach to risk assessment serves to locate accountability in the group rather than in the individual and in this sense interprofessional work may serve as a form of risk insurance for practitioners. Hallett and Stevenson (1980) have argued that the shared decision making of the child protection case conference functions as a device for managing the anxiety of the professionals involved and that this constitutes one of the main arguments for the interprofessional nature of the process.

The involvement of a number of agencies in the planning and delivery of interventions broadens the range of resources available and opens up the possibility of services being delivered in a synchronised manner so that each reinforces the other. For example, child care services might be offered to a mother with mental health problems in a format or frequency which would allow her access to therapeutic help, training or education which would assist with her recovery. Ongoing involvement by a number of professionals will, if coordinated, allow for services to be monitored and progress reviewed across a number of possible outcomes. So, for the mother receiving the package described above, it should be possible for a coordinated interprofessional review to assess improvements (if any) in her mental health, changes in her care of her child and the child's response to substitute care.

The 1999 edition of the *Working together* guidelines (DoH et al, 1999) emphasises the need for interprofessional communication in relation to work that involves risk. Adult mental health services and children's welfare services are exhorted to share information and liaise closely in circumstances where children are perceived to be at risk (DoH et al, 1999, sections 3.45-46). However, as Morrison (2000) has noted, the focus of the guidance is on interagency coordination for those children who are at risk of significant harm. The mechanisms for interprofessional consultation and collaboration in cases where children are judged to be 'in need' are, by comparison, much less clearly specified. The *Framework for the assessment of children in need and their families* (DoH et al, 2000), which, with its emphasis on need rather than protection, applies to a much wider group of families, also stresses the importance of an interagency approach. The framework emphasises that "it is not just social services departments which are the assessors and providers of services" (DoH et al, 2000, p 14). Adult mental health services are described as having a "key role to play" (DoH et al, 2000, p 70) when parents' mental health needs impact on parenting capacity. Primary care team staff are also alerted to their responsibilities to inform child care social work teams of parental problems which may pose risks to children (DoH et al, 2000, p 67).

However, in the absence of child protection case conferences and core groups, the mechanisms for interprofessional work in cases where children are in need remain unclear. Horwath (2002) speculates whether practitioners outside social services departments will be anything but confused about who does what within the assessment framework. Furthermore, a lack of shared understanding concerning other agencies' participation in the framework was noted in a joint monitoring report from the chief inspectors (Chief Inspector of Social Services et al, 2002) on the arrangements for safeguarding children.

The Care Programme Approach (CPA) aims to establish an interagency approach to assessment and planning within adult mental health services. The framework guidance emphasises the need for assessment of both health and social care needs and for health and social services staff to avoid duplicating work (DoH, 1995b, sections 3.1.3-5). Following early research (Schneider, 1993) and reviews of the CPA (SSI, 1996, 1999), there has been increasing emphasis on the integration of health and social services documentation and procedures.

However, there is a considerable gap between providing guidance and tools designed to promote interagency coordination and actually achieving it in practice. Lupton et al (2001) found that different professional groups attached varying levels of importance to such guidance, with social workers, health visitors and the police being more likely to value compliance with central government

to-day agency practice and established procedures suggest that shortfalls in interprofessional communication are often integral to organisations and their operations. For example, the Climbié Inquiry found that hospital social workers did not attend weekly psychosocial meetings at North Middlesex Hospital for a period of three years. These multi-agency meetings were designed to promote the exchange of information between medical staff and social workers.

Despite some warnings concerning the limitations of inquiries as the foundations for building policy (Parker and McCulloch, 1999), they have been enormously influential in the development of child care as well as mental health guidance. Their wide coverage in the media has resulted in pressure on government 'to be seen to do something', and, as noted in Chapter Two, a number of government initiatives aimed at managing risk more effectively can be discerned, particularly in mental health services. Inquiries into homicide have also contributed to a widespread perception that the effectiveness of both child care and mental health services is impeded by problems in interprofessional communication and coordination. This chapter examines the evidence for the effectiveness or otherwise of interprofessional work in both child protection and mental health services before looking at the very limited body of work covering coordination and communication between adult mental health and child care services.

Interprofessional work in child protection

The inquiry into the death of Maria Colwell (DHSS, 1974) was the catalyst for the establishment of Area Review Committees, later redesignated as Area Child Protection Committees (ACPCs). As Chapter Two of this book noted, these interprofessional bodies are responsible for producing local guidance and training aimed at developing coherent and coordinated interprofessional approaches to child protection within a locality. Stevenson (1999) argues that the value of interprofessional work for child protection was well established prior to the Colwell Inquiry. However, the three key features of the child protection system – ACPCs, child protection registers and child protection case conferences – all developed in response to this inquiry, and each is designed to improve coordination between agencies.

The 1980s were characterised by major public inquiries into child deaths which have been exhaustively analysed elsewhere (Stevenson, 1989; DoH, 1991; Corby, 2002). Failures in interprofessional work were a constant theme of these inquiries, with the Jasmine Beckford Inquiry (London Borough of Brent, 1985) highlighting the absence of a coordinated monitoring system between child care social workers, health visitors and teachers. The inquiry report recommended that health authorities should be formally required to report concerns to social services departments. The inquiry into the death of Kimberley Carlile (London Borough of Greenwich, 1987) developed this theme and recommended that a joint agency incorporating both child health and child care social work services be established.

The Cleveland Inquiry (Butler-Sloss, 1988) exposed a complete breakdown in communication between child care social workers and the police, with each service adopting totally uncoordinated responses to the investigation of a large number of cases of sexual abuse diagnosed by paediatricians. In response to this picture, the report aimed to emphasise the joint responsibility of agencies for child protection, asserting that "no single agency – Health, Social Services, Police or voluntary organisation – has the pre-eminent responsibility in the assessment of child abuse generally and child sexual abuse specifically" (Butler-Sloss, 1988, p 248). The Cleveland Inquiry went further than previous reports in advocating the establishment of specialist interprofessional child protection teams, a recommendation that was not implemented but has resurfaced in the Institute for Public Policy Research's proposal for a national child protection service (Kendall and Harker, 2002).

A number of research studies have explored the extent of interprofessional communication and coordination in child protection work. Hallett and Birchall's three-volume study incorporated a literature review (Hallett and Birchall, 1992), a study of professionals' views of interprofessional work (Birchall with Hallett, 1995) and research exploring interprofessional communication and coordination in practice in two research sites (Hallett, 1995). In exploring professionals' views of the child protection system, Birchall and Hallett found that different professional groups varied considerably in their experience of child protection work with some, such as social workers, paediatricians and the police, being heavily involved. Others, such as GPs and teachers, whose responsibilities were targeted on wider populations, were rarely involved and were poorly informed about what might be expected of them. The research found considerable confusion among practitioners concerning other professionals' roles and identified territorial disputes and status differentials as factors that limited collaboration. Hallett's (1995) study of interagency work in practice found that, in the initial stages of a child protection investigation, interprofessional communication and coordination could be fairly well developed, rising to a peak at the initial child protection case conference. However, thereafter other agencies fell away, leaving child care social workers on their own to manage and monitor interventions.

Bannon et al's (1999) study of primary care team members' attitudes towards child protection work identified, like Hallett and Birchall (1992), a lack of engagement with such work on the part of GPs. General practitioners lacked

et al (1999) found that health visitors played a significant role in formal child protection processes and were likely to be involved in sustained joint work with child care social workers. This research, which combined case studies undertaken in three health authority areas with a postal survey of ACPC members in the South West Region of England, also identified low evaluations of accident and emergency (A&E) doctors' performance in child protection from other professionals involved in such work. Hospital doctors emphasised the boundaries of their roles in relation to child protection and were concerned about other professionals' unrealistic expectations of them.

Generally, research into interprofessional work in child protection can be said to have identified failures in communication and collaboration between doctors and child care social workers. While other health professionals such as health visitors and school nurses (singled out in Lupton et al's 1999 study) appear to be recognised as having a significant role in child protection work, medical practitioners, particularly GPs and A&E specialists, are the object of high expectations from other professionals concerning their potential contribution to the child protection process. In practice, however, their input is experienced as disappointing. This mismatch of expectations and performance evaluation derives in part from other practitioners' recognition of the easy and non-stigmatised access which doctors are perceived to enjoy in relation to children's health needs. This is coupled with a failure to acknowledge their lack of time and expertise to pursue child protection issues in depth. However, differentials in status, knowledge base and organisational affiliations also appear to play a part in difficulties in communication and coordination.

The evidence concerning other professionals' experience of difficulties in working with child care social workers identifies differing thresholds of concern as a key issue. Birchall and Hallett (1995) found that health visitors and teachers had a lower threshold for the identification of significant harm than child care social workers and noted that they frequently found the latter unresponsive to cases that they considered warranted immediate intervention. Even after the development of family support services in local authority social services departments, the chief inspectors (Chief Inspector of Social Services et al, 2002) were still reporting that other agencies experienced social services criteria for accepting referrals as being drawn too tightly. Staff shortages among child care social workers were described as resulting in the deployment of inexperienced, temporary staff in intake and duty teams. Other professionals found such workers "impersonal and unresponsive" (Chief Inspector of Social Services et al, 2002, p 47).

The chief inspectors' report (2002) evinces a general lack of confidence in the capacity of ACPCs to deliver coordinated child protection services at the local level. Area Child Protection Committees are described as "weak" and failing to exercise effective leadership (Chief Inspector of Social Services et al, 2002, p 37). The inspectors found that the funding allocated to ACPCs varied considerably, limiting their capacity in some areas. The committees were charged with failing to link up with other key local forums such as domestic violence forums and Multi-Agency Public Protection Panels and with inefficiencies in undertaking Part 8 or serious case reviews. The Climbié Inquiry (Laming, 2003) goes further in advocating that ACPCs, which are criticised for their lack of statutory powers, should be replaced by a Management Board for Services to Children and Families, which would be accountable to a local authority committee. The inquiry report emphasises the need for information about children and families to be freely exchanged between agencies and recommends that government ensures that interprofessional communication is not restricted by legislation on data protection or human rights. Laming's report also proposes a feasibility study on the construction of a national database that would cover all children.

As noted earlier, the death of Victoria Climbié reignited calls for integrated health and social care services for children. Two contrasting models can be identified. The first (Kendall and Harker, 2002) resurrected the proposal mooted in the Cleveland Inquiry for a national child protection agency. This model was strongly opposed by the Association of Directors of Social Services, which argued that such a development would separate the protection of children from family support and so undermine the 'two sides of the same coin' approach that social services had been busy constructing since 1995. The second model proposed the integration of children's services in children's trusts and appeared to offer a structure in which both child protection and family support could be included. At the time of writing, such trusts are still at the blueprint stage, but it seems likely that partnerships developing children's trusts will include health, social care and education services and that there will be considerable variation between local configurations.

Interprofessional work in mental health

Failures in interprofessional and interagency communication and coordination have been a major theme of the stream of inquiries into homicides committed by people with mental health problems. The team reporting on the case of

arliest and most influential

d the main shortcoming in

tion and liaise between all

Christopher Clunis' care

a number of the inquiries

and community services

lnanuy iemale nurses at

iatrist was reinforced by

er. Other professionals,

t also have roles in the

hy somewhere between

hospitals and into the

gers and Pilgrim (2001)

lth practitioners fuelled

nalyses suggest that the

the asylum (Samson,

is usually assigned to a

ker, the lines of case

al responsibility of the

ble to challenge from

light the comparative

practitioners, arguing

3 Mental Health Act

avioural therapy – is

government's proposal

deliver short cognitive

ther dilution of their

siderably, CPNs and

r occupation of the

same professional space in mental health services. The Sainsbury Centre's influential review of the roles and training of mental health staff (Sainsbury Centre for Mental Health, 1997) stopped short of recommending the introduction of a generic community mental health professional. Instead, it proposed core competencies for mental health nurses and social workers which could be developed through joint training and education. The proposals contained in the draft Mental Health Bill (DoH, 2002b) to extend the specialist function of approved social worker (ASW) to other mental health professionals represents a further threat to the distinct identity and role of social workers within mental health services (Stanley and Manthorpe, 2001). As CPNs and mental health social workers are increasingly working in common settings and are employed by the same trusts, the differences in role become harder to discern, although CPNs have retained their hegemony in the administration of anti-psychotic medication in the community.

Despite these conflicts and uncertainties concerning role, most mental health professionals will be working as part of a multidisciplinary team located in a community mental health team (CMHT) a resource centre, or perhaps attached to primary healthcare. In such settings, they will have to reconcile their professional identity with their membership of a team. There has been surprisingly little research conducted on the actual practice of interprofessional work in mental health services. Arguably, the inquiries, with their emphasis on danger and high risk, have been left to fill this vacuum. However, the emergence of CMHTs and joint mental health trusts has produced some evaluative studies that have explored the nature of interprofessional relationships within the new structures.

Øvretveit's (1997) evaluation of a CMHT found that, despite different professionals being located under the same roof, only those service users subject to the aftercare provisions of the 1983 Mental Health Act received effective coordination of their care. Other service users experienced many different reviews from different workers, received conflicting advice and had to repeat the same information to different professionals. Peck et al's (2001) early evaluation of the Somerset Partnerships Health and Social Care NHS Trust found that organisational changes did not as yet seem to have succeeded in creating a new culture which overrode staff's professional attachments.

Accounts of the relationship between specialist mental health services and primary care are even less positive. Jeyarajah Dent and McIntyre's (2000) study of health visitors' experience of working with parents with mental health problems found that the health visitors would have valued support and input from specialist mental health services but encountered reluctance to make referrals to such services from GPs. As the gatekeepers for specialist mental health services, GPs have the power to frustrate the aims of other practitioners who look to them to provide their clients with access to specialist services.

Interprofessional work across the adult–child servi‹
boundary

Falkov's review of 100 Part 8 Reviews found both evidence of parentai ᵐᵉᵗᵃᵐ health needs and "an absence of effective intra and inter agency coordination, collaboration and communication" (1996, p 20). Falkov concluded that child care professionals lacked an understanding of parental mental health needs and that those working in adult services placed little emphasis on child protection and the child's care and welfare. A number of the mental health inquiry reports highlight communication issues across the interface between adult mental health services and child care social work. The inquiry into the care of Darren Carr

protection social workers failure to treat the mental health social workers communication as a referral and noted their "poor understanding of the role of the psychiatric services" (Richardson et al, 1997, p 115).

The inquiry team (Fallon et al, 1999) investigating the allegation that the daughter of an ex-patient had made unsupervised visits to the personality disorder unit at Ashworth Special Hospital found that the hospital social work team there lacked an up-to-date knowledge of child protection procedure. Limited understanding of the roles of staff in agencies working with different user groups and an associated ignorance of relevant guidance informing the work of other services appears to be a key finding of a number of the inquiries covering this interface. In the case of Alfina Magdalena Gabriel, who killed a man she suspected of having previously abused her daughter, the inquiry team (Double, 1998) noted that there had been some communication between professionals but commented that "individual staff having individual inputs did not make a coordinated package" (Double, 1998, p 28). In particular, the report highlighted that the GP played no part in planning the care of mother and daughter. The inquiry also identified failures to hold either a child protection case conference or any other form of multidisciplinary conference to assess risk.

Again, the shortage of published research focusing on interprofessional communication and coordination across the divide between children's and adults' services makes it difficult to gauge the extent to which cases where deaths occur are representative of all work across this boundary. However, accounts which rely primarily on clinicians' case studies (Göpfert et al, 1996) confirm that practitioners in adult mental health services often show no awareness of patients' parental roles and responsibilities. This can apply to social workers as well as to doctors and nurses. Webster et al's (1999) study of mental health social workers' involvement with families looked at the extent to which ASWs engaged with children when parents were assessed for formal admission to hospital. They identified considerable variation in the extent to which ASWs took the children's needs and their response to the assessment into account. The majority of ASWs did not speak to the children in the families.

Hetherington et al's (2001) European study of professional responses to families with mentally ill parents found that workers in mental health services and child welfare workers often misunderstood both the roles and the organisational structures of other agencies. Child welfare practitioners had little knowledge of psychiatric illness and mental health workers lacked a familiarity with child care procedures and local social resources. This resulted in some practitioners having gaps in their knowledge that could contribute to poor assessments of risk. Hetherington et al suggest that routine interagency meetings are effective in building professional confidence in collaboration and increase prospects for interprofessional communication.

The pilot study for the research reported in this book provided a small-scale picture of such interprofessional communication in work where mothers' mental health problems coincide with child care concerns. (This study is discussed in Chapter Five of this book.) However, the research on interprofessional work in this area remains extremely limited. This has resulted in a heavy reliance on the evidence provided by both Part 8 Reviews and mental health inquiries, which has tended to emphasise interprofessional communication as the key to the containment and management of risk. The value of coordinated interprofessional work can be measured more broadly than this. An effective interprofessional approach should be able to deliver interventions that respond to the needs of both parents and children so that meeting one set of needs does not have to be achieved at the expense of the other.

FOUR

The research study

Background to the research

.... understand the response of a range of

from a small pilot study completed in 1997. The results of this pilot led into the design of the main study, which is the focus of the second part of this chapter. The latter sections provide details of the areas included in the study and outline the methodology.

The pilot study

Before embarking on a full-scale research study, we decided to test several of our assumptions, for example, that divides between health and social care, and between children's and adults' services, might affect professional practice with families where mothers had mental health problems. Therefore, we planned and implemented a pilot study (Stanley and Penhale, 1999) designed to examine issues of interprofessional communication and coordination. As this work provided the backdrop to the larger study, it is worth considering it here in some detail.

The pilot study was exploratory in nature and took place in a locality not subsequently used for the main research study. Detailed analysis of 13 families' files was undertaken in one local authority in the east of England. The study explored the nature of serious mental health problems in mothers whose children were on the child protection register, and examined the extent to which different professionals worked together to meet the family's needs.

Each of the families selected for inclusion in the pilot study had been subject to a child protection case conference, and each had one or more child's name included on the child protection register. In all 13 families, which were identified for the pilot study by social work team managers, mothers were considered to have serious mental health problems. Nine of the mothers had been given a formal diagnosis by a psychiatrist and four had been diagnosed by their GPs. Given the predominance of clinical case accounts in the literature on maternal mental health problems (see Göpfert et al, 1996), it appeared valid to examine a small number of cases selected by social workers. However, it must be acknowledged that this was a limited and not necessarily representative sample.

Eight of the 13 mothers in our pilot study were described as depressed – in seven cases the mothers had been allocated a diagnosis of clinical or postnatal depression. This distribution is consistent with national statistics (see Chapter One of this book). However, six of the women were diagnosed as suffering from a personality disorder. In some cases, this diagnosis coexisted with a diagnosis of depression. (Attaching the label 'personality disorder' to mothers with mental health problems requires discussion, and this issue will be addressed in more detail in Chapter Nine of this book.)

When examining the additional problems and circumstances experienced by the 13 mothers in the pilot study, we found five with identified problems of alcohol abuse and two with histories of drug abuse. Three of the women had a partner with a mental health problem and three had a history of childhood sexual abuse. However, the most significant problem, common to all 13, was the experience of domestic violence. Domestic violence appeared to feature significantly in the lives of these mothers with mental health problems and was identified as an issue that would be explored in more depth with the mothers who participated in the main study.

The pilot study found limited involvement from mental health professionals in the cases examined. In nine of the 13 cases, no mental health social worker was involved and in seven cases, no community psychiatric nurse (CPN) was involved. Communication between child care social workers and adult and child psychiatrists was no more than an exchange of letters and reports. The research identified some examples of child care social workers making what were considered inappropriate requests for adult psychiatrists to assess a mother's parenting capacity.

Therefore, interprofessional work was confirmed as a key area for further investigation in our main study, together with exploration of possible differences in professionals' conceptions of need in such families and, where relevant, of significant variations in practitioners' assessments of risk. The study of case files had only addressed professionals' perspectives and it was apparent that these needed to be balanced by the views of service users. The main research study was specifically designed, then, to investigate and incorporate the experiences and perceptions of mothers with mental health problems as well as to explore interprofessional responses to families.

The study areas

The main study was undertaken in two different local authority areas in north-east England, one a unitary authority (A) and the other a metropolitan district (B). The selection of these study sites was in part determined by their interest in the research and the willingness of health and social services to participate, and in part because they were located some distance apart and local service configurations differed. Each area contributed some funding towards the costs of the research. However, the areas were not so totally different from each other in their social and economic levels of need that comparisons are impossible.

Both sites A and B are located in coastal areas and characterised by high levels of unemployment and deprivation (as measured using the Jarman scale), a consequence of the decline of local traditional industries. Neither locality had a significant proportion of individuals from minority ethnic groups within the population. The unitary authority (A) was somewhat larger in terms of

Such problems were intensified by a lack of co-terminosity between health and social services departments. This issue was less of a problem in site A, which was somewhat more 'self-contained'.

The Department of Health's Performance Assessment Framework (PAF) indicators for 1999-2000 (the period when fieldwork was in progress) showed that each authority reported similar levels of performance in terms of the numbers of re-registrations on the child protection register and duration on the child protection register (DoH, 2000b). While each authority was identified as giving rise to some cause for concern on these two measures, both were seen to be improving in these areas. These trends continued in the following year (DoH, 2001) during which the final stage of the research was completed.

While both areas experienced different organisational and service provision changes in health and social care during the period when the study was underway, this was not untypical of many authorities given the modernisation initiatives being widely introduced in response to government directives. Staff in both areas were facing periods of uncertainty and change during the course of the study. Generally, the research findings showed few significant differences between the two areas. Where differences did emerge between the two study sites these are emphasised in the text that follows.

A pluralistic methodology (Stanley et al, 1998) was developed for the study. This approach facilitates the exploration of an issue from a number of different perspectives and allows contrasting voices to be brought together and developed into a dialogue. It also permits a number of methodologies to be brought to bear upon the subject of enquiry. The research aimed to explore practitioners' conceptions of need and their views of their roles and remits in relation to families where mothers' mental health needs coexisted with concerns about significant harm to children. It was agreed that the full range of staff in health, social care and the voluntary sector who were likely to be involved with such families would be included. This would entail substantial numbers of practitioners if all relevant professional groups were to be represented, and a postal survey was identified as the most appropriate method of eliciting their perceptions and experiences. Interprofessional communication and collaboration would be explored through the practitioners' perspectives since any proposals for change in this area would need to be perceived as meeting professionals' diverse needs and interests. In other words, it was acknowledged that practitioners cannot be forced to work together. A postal questionnaire would also allow us to interrogate professionals' views on resources, covering both relevant existing resources and those as yet unavailable in the areas studied. The survey included a mixture of structured and open-ended questions and its design and content were assisted by interprofessional focus groups, which are discussed in full in Chapter Five. The local steering groups, which included agency and user representatives, also contributed to the design of the questionnaire.

For NHS and social services staff, the questionnaire was distributed via internal mailing systems. It soon became apparent that agencies' mailing lists were out-of-date and did not reflect recent staff changes. Considerable work was done to establish which workers were still in post and where. Relevant staff in other agencies were contacted via a series of initial phone calls. In primary care, practice managers emerged as key to achieving GPs' participation in the survey. A second posting of the questionnaire and reminder telephone calls were used to achieve a satisfactory response rate. The SPSS software package, designed for statistical analysis in the social sciences, was used to analyse the data obtained from the survey.

The experiences and perceptions of mothers with mental health problems were explored through a series of individual interviews. By allowing the interviewer to build a rapport with the women, a level of trust arose that facilitated in-depth exploration of sensitive issues. All members of the research team involved in interviewing were qualified practitioners who had experience of working in mental health settings as well as experience of research interviewing. Semi-structured interviews were undertaken with 11 mothers, who were contacted through key informants in health and social services. These women were selected on the basis that they had enduring mental health problems and had experience of a child protection case conference in relation to their children in the last two years. Each of the mothers interviewed was white, of UK origin. This was a reflection of the local populations of the two study sites, which, as was mentioned earlier, had low numbers of individuals from minority ethnic backgrounds. Both study areas, A and B, had very few mental health service users from minority ethnic groups.

Second interviews were completed with five mothers in site A and all three women from site B. Therefore, eight of the 11 women were interviewed twice, with an interval of about six months between interviews. It was envisaged that this would allow sufficient time for the women's mental health condition to change so that the data collected would reflect any such fluctuations. A second interview also allowed for the intervening period to be explored and discussed in depth. Despite numerous telephone calls and follow-up visits, three of the original sample proved either unwilling or inaccessible for the second interview (for example, one woman had moved out of the area).

The women agreed to participate in the interviews, and gave their consent for the interviews to be tape-recorded. Following recording, the tapes of the interviews were transcribed and the mothers were offered the opportunity to receive copies of the transcripts of their interviews. The transcripts were analysed
___ __ _____ _____ _____ _____ to generate sub-themes in line with

formats have been used to deliver the study findings to a range of interest groups. Local advisory groups have played a key role in ensuring local feedback and use of the research. A training package has been developed and delivered in a number of different localities, generally on an interprofessional basis. We will return to discussion of this training course in Chapter Nine of this book, but now we move on in Chapter Five to describe in detail the focus group stage of the study.

FIVE

Identifying key research issues

The focus groups

that addressed the issues tackled

questions for inclusion in the survey of professionals (Dumka et al, 1996). Focus groups have been shown to be particularly effective in accessing members' constructions and attributions of meaning (Bloor et al, 2001), and are thus ideal for testing the acceptability and interpretations of the language used in questionnaires. Since the aim was to develop a survey instrument that was relevant for a variety of professional groups, a range of practitioners needed to be involved in this stage of the study. Given the potentially large number of workers involved in service provision for families where parents have mental health problems, it was not feasible to hold profession-specific groups. Instead, the research team opted for three interprofessional focus groups. These mirrored or approximated the real-life context of case conferences and had the added advantage that they were likely to afford insights into the issues arising for professionals in the practice environment (Kitzinger and Barbour, 1999).

Since the principal reason for holding focus groups was to inform the design of the questionnaire, it was more important for recruitment purposes than is usually the case in focus group research to convene groups that were representative of the wider population to be studied (Bloor et al, 2001). Therefore, the groups involved a range of staff with different professional roles and remits, working in both the statutory and voluntary sector, and with varying levels of seniority and experience. Those recruited included representatives of the following professional groups: child care social workers; health visitors; adult psychiatrists; mental health social workers; community psychiatric nurses (CPNs); children's guardians; practitioners from voluntary organisations serving mental health services users, and from similar organisations for children; and middle managers from both community health and social services.

The focus groups employed a topic schedule. This was designed to move from broad initial questions onto stimulus material that explored perceptions and concerns about risk and diagnosis, and to focus finally on specific aspects of questionnaire design.

Following introductions, each focus group session began with participants wordstorming about the needs of families where the mother had mental health problems and there were child protection concerns (the moderator recording findings on a flipchart). Discussion highlighted several topics, such as the competing demands of individual family members, to which participants were to return in the course of the discussion, and developed, as anticipated, into talk about the possibilities and constraints of service provision in specific geographical areas.

Kitzinger (1995, p 299) has argued that "focus groups reach the parts that other methods cannot reach", and these sessions afforded insights into the complexities of providing care to vulnerable families which could not have been accessed using more structured methods. Since the questionnaire was to explore barriers to interprofessional work, the focus groups were used to examine the ways in which practitioners viewed the remits and responses of colleagues in other professional groups.

Interprofessional communication

The professionals participating in the groups expressed considerable experience of, and disappointment regarding, failures of communication. However, they also engaged in some theorising as to what might give rise to such failures and identified differing notions of confidentiality. They suggested, that, in some circumstances, they themselves might view the exclusive ownership of relevant information as conferring or demonstrating expertise.

> *Child care manager:* "Sometimes it's actually quite difficult to get the correct or accurate information, certainly from the health services − typically, psychiatrists who seem to struggle with the idea of confidentiality and whose confidentiality is being breached and whose responsibility [it is] to have to feed into .... Confidentiality is a sort of barrier .... Psychiatrists and doctors − it's a problem with both. It can prove difficult."

> *Children's guardian:* "The child has to come first − that is often difficult for the doctor to grasp when he has been trained and practised on confidentiality."

> *Child care manager:* "Basic problem is defining who the client is in this context. The family have needs, but, within that, there are a wide range of different needs. It's about unravelling that. We can develop that."

> *Mental health social worker:* "There is also something about ownership of information. Certainly, if you get very sensitive disclosures from adult clients

– 'I got this using my skills that got this information – therefore I'm not going to share it with anybody'." (Focus Group 3)

The topics of communication and confidentiality elicited significant contributions from focus group members: these were salient topics for each member, a fact that gave rise to considerable frustration. On the basis of this stage of the study, it was agreed to incorporate two separate questions in the survey. One asked how frequently individuals experienced problems in coordinating their work with a range of other professionals – including members of their own professional peer group. The issue of confidentiality was addressed ~~common is it for the following groups of~~

were organised and the issue of keyworkers was raised in each group. Although there was broad agreement that this was a good idea, the discussions highlighted a number of problems with the operation of this. It was acknowledged, for instance, that it could be difficult to specify the most appropriate professional group to assume responsibility for this task and also that this could be difficult in relation to specific cases.

Child care social worker: "I don't see how that ever could really happen, having one keyworker, because inevitably, like, child protection working and, sort of, mental health units, you are always going to have two separate workers. To some extent you can't merge them, I don't think, because they are separate and, for instance you know, if sometimes you are in a difficult position, maybe, for instance, as a child care social worker, if the parent wants to talk about their feelings – how they are getting on, that sort of stuff – if you feel that sometimes you have to say, 'Don't talk to me about that – you need to talk to your CPN', but I'm not sure how you get round that."

Mental health social worker: "You can't, because, when the person wants to talk, you've to listen and share, haven't you, because it's at that time...."

Nurse manager: "I'm not sure that you could ever get a system where there was one keyworker."

Mental health social worker: "I can't remember – what's the new jargon they're using?"

Senior mental health nurse: "That's one of the constraints, isn't it? It seems to me those are our needs: to actually, you know, help all these people involved and to work to a particular role and all things that we have to do. But the needs of the family seem to have been left behind. All they really need – from the family's point of view I'm sure that they couldn't give two hoots who their social services keyworker and what the actual name of that person is, their professional rank and things. Only one, as somebody said it there, they need support – somebody to listen to (them) – very simple needs rather than…." (Focus Group 1)

Such excerpts underline the range of meanings and roles that can be attributed to keyworkers by professionals and service users. There is often the problem of concentrating on structural and organisational issues relating to keyworkers to the exclusion of recognising the professional tasks of communicating with and supporting families. Therefore, in order to avoid this problem, it was agreed to ask whether practitioners considered that they had "the scope in (their) job to offer mothers with identified mental health problems adequate opportunities for active listening". A question exploring the issue of whether or not one agency should assume a lead or coordinating role with such families was also included, with the aim of addressing concerns regarding professional communication and coordination.

Assessment of risk

Vignettes involving hypothetical situations (whether fixed, unfolding or systematically varied in specifics of content) have been used in survey research in order to identify and even measure differences in responses to specific scenarios (Finch, 1984). The data produced by focus groups, which can include detailed narrative accounts and case illustrations, can be usefully incorporated into such vignettes. Focus group participants were asked to contribute to designing vignettes that would explore 'typical' challenges involved in work where mental health and child protection issues coincided. While this approach achieved limited success in generating material for potential scenarios, the general discussion in the focus groups did raise some aspects of work with children and parents that merited inclusion in the vignettes. A newspaper clipping with the headline, 'Mother threw baby off bridge' (*The Guardian*, 25 February, 1997), was used to stimulate discussion of concepts of risk and blame. In all three focus groups, participants agreed that reports such as this, which presented professionals as failing to protect children from parents with mental health problems, were regular features of newspaper coverage. In each focus group, more than one member expressed the view that "there but for the grace of God, go I …", emphasising professionals' sense of vulnerability to blame. The newspaper clipping gave rise to broader discussions about the difficulties of assessing risk within a 'blame culture', and of making psychiatric diagnoses in particular. Although professionals had been reluctant to list typical diagnoses or problems when invited to construct a vignette, they concurred that 'personality disorder' (a diagnosis discussed in the newspaper clipping) was a very common, although not very helpful, diagnosis. The following excerpt from one of the focus group discussions demonstrates the imprecise way in which this diagnosis may be used as well as the underlying use to which diagnoses might be put in defining cases as falling within the remit of other healthcare providers or services:

Child care manager: "Personality disorders are untreatable, aren't they?"

Mental health social worker 1: "Oh, no – they are not! Personality disorders can mean all sorts of things. You could have lived next door to somebody with a personality disorder and not know it. What the media would like you to think about a personality disorder is somebody waving an axe above their head. Personality disorder is an umbrella phrase which relates to many symptoms and it is just a way of psychiatrists getting people out of their service, because they feel they can't work with them." (Focus Group 3)

Personality disorders were the diagnosis most frequently singled out for critical discussion by focus group participants. This occurred both in relation to 'directed' comments stimulated by the presentation of our selected newspaper clipping and though 'volunteered' statements arising spontaneously in discussion (the distinction is Becker's, 1977). The attention paid to personality disorder confirmed the view that this would be a useful issue to explore further in the vignettes included in the questionnaire.

The group participants noted how reluctance to call other professionals in could lead to risks being heightened.

"I think, as a child care social worker, I think it would be more helpful if perhaps mental health professionals at an earlier stage in the process would talk about the parenting issues for the children and the family as a whole. At a very early stage, rather than wait until the professional – CPNs or the psychologist – is beginning to get very anxious about the children in the

family and they trigger the child protection system, which [is] too late."
(Child care social worker, Focus Group 2)

Variations between different professionals' assessment of risk in cases of child abuse have been identified by the work of Fox and Dingwall (1985) and Birchall and Hallett (1995). The group participants seemed alert to such differences, both in respect of assessing child care and with regard to establishing the severity and impact of mental health problems on parenting. This indicated that the intended focus on exploring differences between professional groups in terms of how they assessed risk was likely to prove fruitful.

The focus group data also suggested, moreover, that the fluctuating nature of mental health problems may make consistency of assessment even harder to attain as well as presenting services with the challenge of providing a rapid service response:

> "I think that one of the things that happens with the young people that I work with – and it's not only mental illness – it's any parent that has episodic-type illnesses that are really difficult because they can be going along on a kind of even keel and then, all of a sudden, because of whatever the episode is – whether it's a mental health problem or whether it's arthritis – that they physically they can't get out of bed. It's about being those flexible services, being able to respond, because our experience tends to be that by the time the service has been able to be put in place the episode has passed again and the service isn't needed. It's about – yes, that is about care planning – but it's about responsive care planning and response to those sorts of episodic illnesses."
> (Manager of young carers' project, Focus Group 1)

Since it is hard to capture such issues within the scope of structured questionnaires, we opted to ask respondents to comment, via two open-ended questions, on resources that might be valuable for mothers, but which they had difficulty in accessing, and to suggest additional resources not currently available which might be beneficial.

The focus group sessions were used to pilot two open-ended questions relating to the process of referral. These failed to elicit data that had not been generated in response to the other questions on the focus group topic guide and we were satisfied that amendments to the questionnaire would be sufficient to cover this topic. However, there was some discussion concerning how perceived levels of risk might affect a practitioner's ability to refer mothers with mental health problems to other services. A child care social worker noted that "it's getting your particular client higher up on the priority list", while a mental health social worker commented on the way in which mothers with mental health problems could be excluded from services:

> "Some of the more specialist services for maybe some of the younger mothers who have mental health problems, they want access but they can't have access

because they have got mental health problems." (Mental health social worker, Focus Group 3)

While mental health needs were perceived as excluding some women from mainstream services, some professionals acknowledged that they had on occasion over-emphasised the degree of risk to a family in order to access services. It was decided, therefore, to include this as a fixed-choice question in the survey.

The focus group stage of the study provided some useful data on interprofessional communication and issues of risk assessment (see Barbour et al, 2002). It also proved a valid approach to development of the survey instrument, the relevance and salience of questions

SIX

Mothers' perspectives

Constructing the sample

... interviews undertaken with mothers with mental

aftercare form (Green and Hyde, 1997). Our study aimed to interrogate service users' experience of both mental health and child care services in more depth and to examine need alongside attitudes to services.

For this stage of the research, health and social services staff in the two study sites were asked to identify mothers whose children had been the subject of a child protection case conference in the previous 18 months and who had a diagnosis of mental illness. This could be a diagnosis provided by any health professional and could include diagnoses of personality disorder and repeated episodes of self-harm, but not diagnoses of substance misuse alone. Fewer interviews took place in site B, despite repeated attempts by local practitioners to recruit appropriate interviewees for the study. In this area, in particular, a number of practitioners from different agencies identified the same women as potential participants: this might be explained by the smaller size of the locality.

A total of 11 women were interviewed across both sites using a structured interview schedule devised by the research team. This schedule was developed with the help of the project advisory groups in each site. Representatives from service user groups were included on both steering groups, and their comments were particularly valuable in relation to the development of these interview schedules. An initial pilot interview was completed with one mother and the schedule was refined in the light of her feedback.

A second series of slightly less structured interviews was undertaken after a period of at least six months. A total number of eight second-stage interviews were completed. Three of the original sample proved unwilling to be interviewed or inaccessible (one having moved out of the area). Eight of the original 11 women were living in site A and three in site B. It was clear that the women shared many of the issues that were raised, and location did not seem to be significant in determining their responses. The quotations used in this chapter and in Chapter Seven will not be ascribed to particular individuals or their location in order to protect the anonymity of the women involved.

Mothers' characteristics

The 11 women participating in the research were aged between 26 and 37, with the median age of the group being 32. Only four were living with a partner, although another two had a non-resident partner. Three were currently married; thus, seven of the women were 'lone parents'. Although lone parenthood is not necessarily problematic, for women it is frequently accompanied by a constellation of social problems, including poverty, poor housing and social exclusion (Hills, 1998). Life on the margins of society, with significant levels of financial difficulties and perhaps also a lack of appropriate support networks, is frequently stressful. Lone mothers are the group most likely to manifest generalised anxiety disorder (ONS, 2000) and the high rates of depression in this group were discussed in Chapter One of this book. Although some of the women in our study described receiving support from friends, or families, the interviews also provided accounts of difficulties in family relationships and quite high levels of conflict.

Clearly, the type of support that a close relationship with a resident partner may afford was not a reality for the majority of women in the group. It is important to recognise that a number of the women encountered problematic, even abusive relationships with partners, and any idealisation of the intimate partner relationships the women had experienced had to be avoided. A number of partners (past and present) were described by the women as abusive and violent:

> "In the past, my husband was violent. I was scared – people used to tell me to leave – I was just too scared. I still get letters and cards asking me to come back."

> "I seem to attract men like that – there's been a few.... It makes me feel depressed – sometimes, I wonder if I deserved what I got."

The high levels of exposure to violence in the domestic setting experienced by women with mental health difficulties has been identified elsewhere (Sheppard, 1997) and was also found in the pilot study preceding this research (Stanley and Penhale, 1999). Likewise, studies of women experiencing domestic violence show high rates of mental health problems, particularly depression (Cascardi et al, 1999; Golding, 1999). Humphreys and Thiara (2003) explore the processes through which male strategies of control and violence erode self-esteem and contribute to anxiety and panic attacks. High levels of violence and conflictual relationships appeared to be almost the 'norm' for many of our sample. Sheppard and Kelly (2001, p 77) describe such violence as characteristic of the "fractured relationships" experienced by many of the women in their study. This term would appear to be relevant for the mothers participating in this study also.

While some of the relationships that the women experienced were – or had been – with violent partners, in other relationships the men were described as unreliable and in some ways dependent on the women. This was attributed to a range of problems; for example, a number of male partners were reported to have substance misuse problems (drug or alcohol related) or their own mental health difficulties.

Financial problems were evident for all the mothers interviewed. Indeed, for this group of women, financial difficulties were extensive and were the most

children in securing a right to council accommodation. A number of the women reported that, following their children being taken into local authority care, they had lost their council housing. Privately rented accommodation could be in poor states of repair and in more deprived areas. The women described themselves as unhappy with this situation, but were unable to seek better housing due to high levels of financial difficulties. The mothers seemed to have much in common with the lone mothers studied by Targosz et al (2003), who found a strong association between depression and poverty. The majority of women with mental illness included in their study were unemployed and lived in rented accommodation. A combination of poverty, accommodation problems and relationship difficulties seemed likely to have contributed to and exacerbated the mental health problems experienced by the mothers in this study.

The size of the women's families ranged from one to six children, with four of the 11 women having four or more children. Family size can also contribute to poverty. Larger family size may play a part in the aetiology of mothers' mental health problems; the mother's role in a large family may be more demanding, with adverse effects for coping capacity and self-esteem. Brown and Harris' (1978) classic study of working-class women in Camberwell, London, identified larger families as a vulnerability factor for depression. Larger numbers of children, coupled with a reliance on state benefits or low levels of income and poor accommodation, can produce high levels of deprivation, impoverishment and stress. At the time of interview, the majority of women in this study no longer had all their children living with them, as Table 6.1 shows.

Eight of the women had at least some of their children looked after or adopted. Of these, a majority had all their children living away from them.

Table 6.1: Current location and status of children

	Number of families
All children looked after/adopted	5
Some children looked after/adopted	3
No children looked after/adopted	3

However, a small number currently had all their children living with them. Those mothers with only one child were more likely to have that child living with them, suggesting that those women with smaller families were better able to cope or to maintain a level of care acceptable to social services.

In terms of their mental health conditions, all the women in the study had at least one mental health diagnosis and three of the group reported two diagnoses. A psychiatrist had conferred the majority of these diagnoses. However, three of the women identified a GP as the source of their diagnosis. The diagnoses as reported by the women are listed in Table 6.2.

One woman reported the rather non-specific diagnosis of 'mental health problem'. This may reflect a reluctance to 'own' a diagnosis or non-specific information from health professionals. A slight majority of the women had diagnoses that involved affective disorders, either depressive illnesses or bipolar disorders. This is in keeping with epidemiological studies concerning women's mental health, as noted in Chapter One.

Stress factors

Six of the 11 women reported no other major health problems of significance, but four mentioned asthma or chest problems as causing some concern. These types of illness may be related to poverty and poor housing conditions. Social isolation also affected three women who reported that they did not have access to well-developed support networks. Financial difficulties can restrict social networks as there may not be sufficient income for a family to afford leisure activities, transport or communication costs. Targosz et al's (2003) study of lone mothers with mental illness found that two thirds had no access to a car.

Issues relating to loss constituted another major source of stress. Loss and bereavement were relevant factors for the majority of the group: eight of the 11 women had experienced significant bereavements. In three of these cases, this involved the recent death of their own mother. One mother in the sample,

Table 6.2: Diagnosis as reported by mothers

Depression	3
Manic depression	2
Psychotic disorder	3
Personality disorder and schizoid disorder	2
Mental health problems	1

who had lost three close relatives in the space of a year, saw these multiple bereavements as playing a part in the development of her own mental health problems:

> "I went off course when he died. I was going downhill – just my way of trying to cope with myself.... I just used to sit there and cry all the time."

Bereavement through the death of a significant other appeared to be implicated in the mental health problems of a number of the women. There were also other areas of loss, however, that impacted on their lives. We noted above that

role was also difficult for the

shall see in Chapter Seven.

Additionally, a number of the women experienced different types of loss in other areas. Almost half of the women did not have a current partner and a small number reported a succession of unsuccessful relationships: the loss of a long-term positive relationship was keenly felt in a number of cases. The three women who had had established networks and then lost them for a variety of reasons also experienced social isolation and lack of social supports as significant losses. Five of the women had children who were disabled. The range of disabilities experienced by the children included epilepsy, speech problems and learning difficulties. Two of these women expressed substantial feelings of loss in relation to this disability. Six women described other difficulties experienced by their children, including emotional and behavioural problems and violent behaviour. Three women indicated that their children's difficulties had meant that they were not able to have outside social relationships or activities as they might have wished, irrespective of any financial considerations.

Support systems

One of the areas explored with the women during interview was the issue of support systems and how these might assist and enable families. For the purposes of the study, support systems were defined as networks of friends or family members that the women could draw on for help. For many mothers, the presence of such a support network acts as a protective factor, helping to create a buffer against the longer-term effects of stress. The role played by supportive relationships has been explored in some depth through Brown's work on depression (Brown and Harris, 1978; Brown et al, 1986).

For many mothers, other family members provide the fundamental basis of this support, which may be both instrumental (practically based) and expressive (emotionally based) in its forms. In exploring support systems, it was notable that only four women said that they had any family members living nearby. This clearly limited the amount of support that was easily available to them. However, when family support was accessed, it was valued:

> "You know, if I've got a problem with social workers and that, I normally go to me brother's and chat with me brother and get his advice and stuff like that, or talk to his wife 'cos she seems to be good...."

The six women who had a current partner described them as supportive. As one woman stated:

> "He throws out my razor blades. He's there when I need to talk to him."

Another commented:

> "He tells me he wants me to get fully better."

However, in three cases, the partners had their own mental health problems, which might have limited the amount of support available at certain points in time. Two women described their partner's problems as stress inducing, as the following comment illustrates:

> "He wants a lot of attention. Sometimes he tires me out when I'm trying to sort my house out or trying to be on time for contact or decisions."

Partners and relatives were the people most likely to be seen as providing a close and confiding relationship. Three women were unable to identify anyone who offered this level of support and consequently experienced high levels of social isolation. Sheppard and Kelly (2001, p 77) characterise difficulties in, or lack of, wider relationships as a further dimension of the "fractured relationships" that many of the women in their study experienced. In our study, a similar pattern in social support networks was evident.

Experiences of mental health services

Each of the women had experience of in-patient treatment in a psychiatric unit. Eight had been admitted compulsorily, as involuntary patients, under the 1983 Mental Health Act. Table 6.3 shows that the majority of the women had three or more admissions to hospital: these included voluntary and involuntary admissions. This suggests that their mental health problems were, or had been, severe. For a number of the women, the ability to access hospital-based care on an informal and voluntary basis was an important indicator that they were

Table 6.3: Mothers' experiences of psychiatric admission

One admission only	3
Three admissions	5
>Three admissions	3

managing their conditions. In outlining their mental health history, all but one of the women described a gradual onset of mental health problems. Six of the women reported their problems emerging before the age of 14.

The women's personal histories gave some insight into the childhood

In this study, those women who had experienced abuse in childhood perceived this to be a major contributory factor in the development of their mental health problems. A number of the women also saw their early experience of abuse as exacerbating their continuing difficulties in adulthood. Many of these experiences were spoken about at length and with evident distress during interview. Several of the mothers interviewed made connections between their abusive experiences in childhood and their behaviour as adults. One woman stated:

> "I wanted help with the kids but ex-husband wouldn't have it. He used to abuse me constant.... He used to hit kids real hard. I was abused when younger over time in my own family."

Another commented:

> "I was abused from 11-14 by my brother – sexually abused. Son was abused at six – he's in care now.... I was scared and coped by cutting – my release. I OD'd loads of times ... never had any family help."

The woman quoted below also considered that her experiences of abuse had shaped child care social workers' attitudes to her as a parent:

> "Have had depression all my life and been linked up with social services all my life. Social services have been concerned about my abilities to cope 'cos I was bashed up myself as a kid – it's affected me as an adult.... Psychiatrists say: 'That's your past, don't live in it', but it comes up in meetings with social workers."

Table 6.4: Mothers' personal histories

Abused as a child	10
Domestic violence	8
Personal experience of care systems	4

Bifulco and Moran (1998) suggest that earlier experiences of abuse may affect an individual's ability to deal with challenges occurring later in life. As noted earlier, abusive experiences had continued into adulthood for eight of the women who reported domestic violence from their partner or former partners. One woman clearly attributed her own problems to her partner's violence:

> "He used to 'bray' me. It was too much for him – kids, me, the house. He used to take it out on me. Twenty per cent of my breakdown's due to him."

Sheppard's (1997, p 99) account of depressed mothers "living in families pervaded by abuse and violence" seems to be of particular relevance here.

While a history of childhood abuse was the experience most frequently cited by the women as the cause of their mental health problems, other contributory factors were identified as significant (Table 6.5). It is relevant to note that two mothers felt that they had not been offered sufficient help with the children when they had needed it. In addition, these women considered that losing the care of their children had exacerbated their mental health problems.

Only two of the women acknowledged having current problems with alcohol or drugs, although three admitted to having had such difficulties in the past. In terms of prescribed drugs, three of the group were not taking any medication at the time of the first interview. Most were taking either anti-depressants, anti-psychotic medication, anxiolytics or mood stabilisers; some were taking a combination. At the time of the second interview, two women expressed a wish to manage without medication and linked this with a desire for normality.

Since each the women had experience of in-patient care, they were able to provide some valuable insights concerning the experiences of parents who are admitted to psychiatric hospitals. Only three out of the 11 mothers reported

Table 6.5: Mothers' perceptions of factors contributing to mental health problems

	Mentions
Childhood abuse	10
Long history of depression/worrying	4
In care as a child	3
Domestic violence	2
Losing care of children	2
Did not get any help with caring for children	2

that their children had been present at the time of their admission: of these three, only one considered that no one had explained to the children what was happening. In most cases, the children were looked after by social services while their mother was in hospital (in three families, the children were already being looked after at the time of their mother's admission to hospital). Three mothers indicated that their own mothers or the children's fathers had cared for the children during their admissions. All but two of the mothers had had some form of ongoing contact with their children while they were in hospital. The majority had found this contact unsatisfactory and problematic. A number of different reasons for this were cited, including feelings of frustration that

children at that time. Mothers also described

and Welsh Office, 1999, section 26.3).

The mothers described the impact that their status as a psychiatric patient had on them as a parent. Feelings of failure as a parent were apparent:

"The kids kept saying: 'Why are you in here?' Trying to explain was upsetting. I thought: 'I shouldn't be in here – why can't I be like other mums out there?'"

However, for three of those interviewed, there was an acknowledgement that hospital admission offered some sense of security and relief from pressures of, and a sense of, not coping:

"It felt strange. I wasn't used to being there. I felt safe – it was better for the children."

At the time of the second interview, some of the women described the stigmatising effects of being labelled as a psychiatric patient:

"I won't go back and be under any doctor or psychiatric-wise.... You get branded again all over, and nine times out of 10 it will be a new one. They label, they try and find an excuse to give you labels and when you haven't been back for four or five years and you suddenly go back after that length of time, you get a new label, you know, and then they'll think the tablets are not working, so how about a stay in hospital to give you a rest, that doesn't improve anything at the end of the day.... You get sucked into the system...."

For this woman, contact with psychiatric services had the effect of confirming her unsuitability as a parent in the eyes of social services. Therefore, she was adamant that, while she might use the services available at her GP's surgery, she would avoid contact with specialist mental health services, as she considered that this would almost inevitably lead to further difficulties.

Nearly every one of the women interviewed reported fears that they might lose their children as a result of their mental health problems (either directly or indirectly). A third of the women said that this perception had affected their willingness to seek help, generally in a negative way. This view was summed up by one woman, who said:

> "That's why I won't always ask for help. I'm worried that they will come and take them off me."

Effects on children

During the interviews, the women were asked to talk about what they considered to be the effects of their mental health problems on their children. The majority of the women were able to acknowledge that their problems had impacted on their children. A number of the women described their children taking on parenting or caring responsibilities:

> "They have seen the effects of me cutting. How I have harmed myself – left mental scars. Mainly on the oldest one. He doesn't talk about it – just gets on with things. Even when he was in care, he used to come home from school to see how I was. Felt responsible for me. He grew up too soon."

Four of the six mothers who had children living at home with them acknowledged that the children had had to help more in the home as a result of their mental health problems. Some of the women were also aware that their children had been distressed or frightened by their behaviour:

> "At first it was scaring my kids – they didn't know what I would say next.... Children were frightened and then got used to it."

Six of the women reported that their children had received or were receiving help in their own right. The types of help that the children received varied from psychological and psychiatric services to participation in a young carers' group. However, it was notable that three of these six women felt that they had little information about the actual help that their children were receiving. This was explained in part by the fact that, in some cases, children were living elsewhere. Nevertheless, such feelings also seemed to reflect the mothers' sense of not being involved in, or of being excluded from, aspects of their children's lives. This view anticipates the theme of partnership considered in Chapter Seven, which addresses the mothers' evaluations of interventions and services.

SEVEN

The mothers' evaluations of professional support

This chapter examines the mothers' evaluations of professional intervention.

Experience of child protection system

The routes by which the families had come to the attention of child care social work varied. Three women described social work involvement commencing late in pregnancy or soon after birth, three others indicated that various individuals or professionals had referred them to child care social work, while two reported contact with the service as dating from the time of psychiatric admission. Although two of the mothers acknowledged that they had needed help at that point, five had felt angry and had found the involvement intrusive:

> "It wasn't nice: I felt really angry. I said I'd never touch my kids, and then teatime I got a knock from the social worker."

> "I hated it – it was just interfering and trying to run my life for us."

Most of the women in the sample considered that they had had little power over the events that had taken place once the process had commenced. The investigations that followed initial contact with social services evoked feelings of a loss of control, or of being judged:

> "Social services want you to sign things – don't read out the small print. I didn't understand; no time to see a solicitor."

"You get the feeling all the time you're being watched. Makes you feel inadequate – saddened that they didn't trust us. I was never trusted as a kid neither."

The sense of loss of control expressed by the mothers seemed to have been experienced from the early stages of their contact with the child protection system and, as discussed later in this chapter, informed the mothers' views about working in partnership with professionals. This sense of having little or no power mirrored the mothers' wider experiences: a number described their lives as chaotic and beyond their control. Sheppard and Kelly (2001) identified similar feelings in the mothers in their study and they speculate that the consequent experience of powerlessness on involvement in the child protection system may induce or exacerbate depression.

Ten of the women had attended either case conferences or review meetings relating to the care of their children. The majority of the mothers had someone with them to offer support during such meetings. Where this person was a professional, he or she was likely to be a mental health social worker or a mental health resource centre worker. However, even when such support was available to the women, half of the group described such meetings as threatening or intimidating:

"Meetings were very threatening because it felt as though they made all the decisions: 'You agree, don't you?' It felt very dictatorial in a way."

Two women felt that their presence had effectively not even been acknowledged within the meetings:

"Quite hard – I felt they were speaking saying I wasn't there, but I was."

"Upsetting where they was talking about the kids. Looking at the report – I just get more upset."

Two of the mothers reported that they had eventually stopped attending such meetings. This appeared, at least in part, to be due to the women's views that their contribution would not make any difference and reflected their sense of an inability to really contribute to and influence such situations:

"I didn't always go. I left them to it. I knew what they were going to say."

Farmer and Owen (1995) and Cleaver and Freeman (1995) have described similar responses to involvement in the child protection system. Their studies did not focus solely on the experiences of parents with difficulties relating to mental health, but the findings resonate with the experiences of these mothers. Although these and other studies which were carried out in the late 1980s and early 1990s resulted in renewed emphasis in policy guidance on working in partnership with families (DHSS Inspectorate, 1995), child protection procedures continued to be experienced by these mothers as entailing a loss of control and powerlessness. Sheppard (2002) suggests that depressed mothers may be particularly vulnerable to the coercive aspects of the child protection system and may not be able to use opportunities for partnership. However, the women in our study were able to identify the gaps between the rhetoric of partnership and its practice:

> "The social services keep talking about shared care. If they want to do that, then fine, someone within that shared care basis should inform me whatever

placed on the register. In eight cases, the mothers thought that their children's names had been removed from the register by the time of the interview.

Each of the women had experienced court proceedings in relation to their children. The majority of these cases had been care proceedings, but two had been in relation to adoption and three cases involved either contact or residence orders or determinations of parental responsibility. Six of the group described the experience of court proceedings as 'horrible', 'scary' or 'stressful'. As one woman stated:

> "I felt I was being punished just for being ill."

However, three of the group found the experience 'not too bad', with one woman reporting a sense of relief in response to the court's decision. For this woman, who reported that she had not been able to cope with her children at that particular point in time, the fact that this was acknowledged within the court setting had been of some benefit to her.

Just under half of the women expressed feelings of being blamed for their child care problems. Irrespective of whether they were or had been responsible for these difficulties, this perception of blame seemed to adversely affect the women and meant that they were less likely to be able to resolve their problems in a positive way. A small number of the women felt that they were victims of the system, either because they felt that they had been inappropriately accused in relation to the 'offence', or because they considered they had been allocated responsibility for their partner's behaviour. (In one situation, for example, the children's names remained on the child protection register after the abuser had left the home.)

We noted in Chapter Six that fears of losing their children limited the mothers' readiness to use services. They also acknowledged a reluctance to be open and honest, particularly in their dealings with child social workers who were perceived as controlling and wielding considerable power. Mothers feared that, were they to say too much about their ongoing difficulties or other incipient problems, this could lead to the removal and loss of their children:

> "That's why I won't ask for help. I'm worried that they will come and take them off me. I talk to the mental health resource centre workers mostly...."

While avoidance of this eventuality was clearly of key importance to the women, it meant that social workers were deprived of information that might have been relevant to an assessment of the children's needs. It was also evident that a number of the women were not fully able to acknowledge or accept messages of support from their social workers as they were only aware of the power differentials and the implicit threat to the family from involvement with child protection systems.

Parenting at a distance

As we saw in Chapter Six, eight of the 11 women had at least some of their children looked after or adopted. Of these eight, five had all their children living away from them at the time of the interviews and, for this group of women, this was an established, long-term situation. Between them, the women had their children cared for in the full range of alternative settings, including residential care, care with relatives or friends and foster care (the most frequently cited setting). They had mixed experiences of these placements: one woman reported that one of her children had experienced abuse in care, and a number of the women described difficulties in relation to foster carers. Such difficulties involved either the breakdown of these placements or their own lack of involvement in the arrangements for the care of their children.

Three of the eight women thought that they had sufficient contact with the children that were not living with them. Overall, the experience of contact in the different settings was quite diverse, with only two of the mothers completely positive about the arrangements for contact. Two of the mothers found the separation at the end of a contact session to be 'distressing' or 'heartbreaking'. Several of the women seemed to consider conditions for contact to be unacceptable, especially when children were in residential care. This was to be particularly the case where the contact was either infrequent or was supervised. One woman who had a child in a residential placement in another county reported:

> "When I've been down they've supervised, but that doesn't feel nice – they're just sat there watching you. I got quite angry with one who followed me upstairs when contact was in my own home."

Contact was important to the mothers who all saw themselves as continuing to play an important role in their children's lives. This was evident even when, as in at least one situation, there appeared to be little realistic hope of the children returning to live at home again.

Views of foster parents varied, but there was some resentment expressed concerning the material resources that the foster parents were able to provide for children. Two of the women noted that financial support appeared to be available for foster carers that they themselves would have appreciated and felt they would have benefited from:

all the activities for

experienced in providing

distant from them. Remaining involved and maintaining involvement in the absence of children from the family home proved demanding and exacting. Such difficulties seemed to be particularly evident in relation to adolescents:

> "Like they come in and like, they like, they rule me and tell me what to do, and I'm thinking 'They shouldn't be doing that'. I don't know because with them not being with me ... they come in and think 'I can rule me mam, me mam gives in'."

The issue of co-parenting alongside others is an area where additional support and improved liaison might well be both welcomed and effective. Given the likelihood that at least some of these children would return home in the long term (Bullock et al, 1993), such input could be regarded as a valuable investment. The mother quoted immediately above appeared to be very keen to have more feedback on her children's behaviour and progress in foster care but reported that she had found it difficult to access this:

> "Like when they're bad ... they say, 'Get in touch with the carers', and the carers say, 'Get in touch with the social worker', I'm like that.... And I feel just a bit, you know, a waste of time − 'cos I'm back and forwards."

Although seven of the women felt that they were involved in ongoing decisions about their children's care, they also considered that the level of involvement varied considerably between different settings. There were reports that some residential and foster carers provided much more information and feedback than others. While this is understandable and perhaps to be expected, it also led to frustration and confusion for the women, particularly for those mothers who had several children who were being cared for in a number of different settings.

Contact with other professionals

The women were asked to comment on the number of professionals they were currently seeing. Mothers had involvement from a wide range of professionals: child care social workers, GPs, mental health social workers, mental health resource centre workers and adult psychiatrists were the professional groups most frequently mentioned. The mothers listed between two and nine professionals whom they were currently in contact with.

It was notable that none of the women thought that too many organisations or individuals were involved. Indeed, those women who felt that there were too few professionals involved tended in fact to have a high number of professional contacts (between five and seven individuals identified). A wider range of contacts (between two and nine individuals) was found for those women who described the amount of involvement as 'just right'. The significant factor determining the level of satisfaction with the amount of agency support that was available seemed more likely to be the women's own level of need rather than the actual number of agencies involved.

The second set of interviews provided evidence that the women were well able to differentiate between the various professional organisations and their roles, and that they were not confused about who provided what service. While there were concerns reported about having to repeat concerns to a number of different professionals, the women also evinced some anxiety about professionals passing information between themselves:

> "There is a difference between social services and their client and two professionals together speaking about you. Things get side-tracked and information gets passed over and sometimes it gets confused and muddled up."

The mothers were also asked to indicate who had been of most assistance to them, in both past and present terms. The professional groups most frequently cited as the most helpful were mental health social workers and mental health resource centre workers. Additionally, psychologists in adult mental health services who took on a therapeutic role were often rated as most helpful. A key factor in determining a professional's perceived usefulness was the mother's sense that these workers were available and 'there for them':

> "My keyworker at the mental health resource centre – 'cos she is there – I can phone her up. She says ring me up if you need me."

The women also emphasised the presence or absence of listening skills in professionals and the importance of practitioners being caring or responsive to their feelings. Understanding and non-judgmental attitudes were also valued:

"[The mental health social worker] explained a lot about my illness and didn't judge me. Treated me as a human being and was very encouraging and supportive – she's got time for you."

In contrast, the two professional groups most frequently identified as least helpful – GPs and child care social workers – were criticised by the women for both a lack of accessibility and also of understanding:

"The GP doesn't seem to listen to what I'm saying – he rushes."

The women's positive evaluation of professionals who were 'there for me' was further strengthened and reiterated in the second set of interviews:

"When I get down, right down ... I want somebody, I don't know, to talk to...."

The concept of 'being there for me', encompasses availability, listening and a commitment to the service user as an individual. The significance attached to this concept by the mothers may contribute to their low evaluation of child care social work. As Chapter Eight shows, a comparatively high proportion of child care social workers responding to the survey said that they did not have opportunities for active listening in their work. The mothers participating in Sheppard and Kelly's (2001) study also reported that child care social workers offered little in the way of emotional support.

The value of non-judgmental attitudes was explored further in the second interview and the contribution of such attitudes in relation to keeping families together was emphasised:

"It's non-judgmental ... that they don't think anything less of me because you know, you're having a difficult period or you're having a bit of trouble at the moment. They don't instantly ring the alarm bells and say, 'Oh, you're not coping' and need to get social services involved and get her back into care and things like that."

Trust

In the second set of interviews, the importance of being able to trust professionals emerged as a clear theme. It was evident that, in part, trust derived from the availability of professionals:

> "So that's why I trust me solicitor because he's there for us all the time."

Problems in contacting child care social workers could be experienced by the women as disempowering and underlined the sense of lack of control that most of the women experienced. Delays in visits by child care social workers, difficulties in making contact with them, or uncertainties as to whether messages were conveyed to the right people, could lead to much frustration for mothers and perceptions of lack of involvement or even respect from individual workers. Although some of the women expressed very negative views about child care social workers, a number mentioned that they would like more contact with these workers. This may have reflected an attempt to achieve more involvement with their children if they were looked after, but may also have been an expression of a need for more support. Indeed, those women who received social work support from mental health social workers or mental health resource centre workers felt that the specific focus on their needs, as distinct from a concern with those of the children, was beneficial. Child care social workers' necessary focus on the children was, in some cases, perceived as excluding the women and as marginalising them. Some of the women thought that a child care social worker could not adequately relate to them as individuals in their own right.

Trust was also conceived of as founded in reciprocity:

> "I like to see someone I can trust because of all the broken promises...."

> "If they're not being straight with you, how can you be straight with them?"

Hetherington et al's (2001) research on a range of professionals in Europe also emphasised the importance of trust in the relationship between mothers with mental health problems and health and social care services. When trust breaks down, the relationship can become adversarial, if not openly antagonistic. This was particularly evident in the way some of the women characterised their relationships with child care social workers:

> "She's on the other side though 'cos she works for social services."

> "They tried to shut doors on us and that, but I was ready to kick them back open and I thought, 'Well, I'm not giving up. I've had enough with social services'."

"They've never played it fair so no arrangement has really worked, because they've never played it fair with me."

From the women's perspective, the hostility they expressed towards child care social work was matched by a lack of information concerning their children from carers and social workers. For instance, in the course of a crisis arising with her son's residential placement, one mother found:

"I'm sitting here all week twiddling me thumbs and the social worker says he would ring us back ... and he never did so."

when you're away?'.... I'm told, 'Sorry, he's away, he'll not be in until such-and-such', and I've got to wait all that time to try and sort it out."

One woman described in detail the impact that a loss of trust had on her communication with child care social workers:

"Social services still say to this day if I end up in hospital ... I'd lose the kids. So that hangs over your head – it makes you stay quiet rather than say anything at all.... It's been said I don't give social services enough information on a regular basis – I've been put down as uncooperative – a nightmare where social services are concerned."

The breakdown in communication noted here was described by a number of the women as characterising their relationships with child care social workers or child care settings. The mothers participating in Nicholson et al's (1998) US study expressed a similar reluctance to use services where it was considered that this might be seen to reflect on their parenting capacity. It is apparent that the cost of this breakdown in trust is that mothers themselves may not receive the support they need prior to a crisis occurring and professionals' ability to assess risks for the children may be compromised by lack of information. Furthermore, a lack of compliance on the part of mothers may be interpreted negatively by child care social workers and contribute to the likelihood of mothers losing care of their children.

While the women were able to acknowledge that they had, on occasion, found child care social workers helpful and were able to respect individual child care workers who were perceived to be 'fair', the overall view of child care social work was of a failure of partnership. The relationship with this service was frequently characterised as one in which trust was absent, communication was poor, professionals were inaccessible and the women felt judged and under scrutiny. While GPs were also viewed as unhelpful, the criticisms were confined to their lack of availability, understanding and communication skills. Since they were not perceived to control the women's access to their children in the way that child care social workers were, they were experienced as less threatening and the relationship was therefore not depicted as adversarial or conflictual.

By contrast, those professionals such as mental health social workers, mental health resource centre workers, psychologists, community psychiatric nurses and counsellors were more likely to be perceived as helpful. This assessment was linked with their capacity for listening and 'being there' for the women, together with non-judgmental attitudes. These were the relationships that the women were most likely to experience as therapeutic, perhaps because in the context of a trusting relationship they were able to acknowledge their own vulnerability. The account below conveys clearly the role of a therapeutic relationship based on trust in resolving past trauma and promoting self-esteem:

> "I opened up in front of me counsellor and she got us help from the council and I opened up all about me past and the more I talked about it, the more strong I felt inside, that I could handle it and I could open up instead of feeling guilty.... It helped me in so many ways and that's because it made me come out of me shell where I could stand up for meself and say 'Look! It's me!'"

Interestingly, although a significant number of the women were seeing psychiatrists at the time of the study, they were not viewed as positively as these other mental health professionals. For these women, psychiatrists were experienced as remote and usually male authority figures who might confirm their incompetence as a parent, an incompetence they feared would be communicated to child care social services. Therefore, contact with psychiatry was seen as best avoided, as this would almost inevitably lead to further difficulties over time.

The experiences of intervention reported by the mothers seemed to be associated with the degree to which they felt either supported and included or ignored and excluded from different systems. Clearly, the extent to which professionals could wield formal coercive powers in relation to the mothers and their children was relevant to these assessments, but the attitudes and availability of the practitioners were also of importance here. The question of whether practitioners considered themselves able to offer the services that women wanted will be discussed in Chapter Eight.

EIGHT

The professionals and their practice

The sample

local services. ~~rostai questionnaires~~

practitioners and middle managers, staff in voluntary organisations, including children's guardians (formally known as Guardians ad Litem), and police officers with responsibilities for child protection. Professionals were included in the survey on the basis of their involvement in work with families where mental health needs and child care concerns coincided and according to the perceived relevance of the research to their core business. Some professionals, such as teachers, were excluded since they only occasionally work with whole families with mental health needs and the survey was not considered to be sufficiently germane to their core task (see Birchall with Hallett, 1995). A group of residential child care workers who undertook outreach work with families were included in the survey in site B as their experience appeared relevant.

The 500 practitioners (327 in Site A and 173 in Site B, the smaller site) who responded to the survey from both areas covered a wide range of professionals (Table 8.1). As in any locality, the different groups are not equally represented, but the power wielded by any one profession within a local network derives less from their numbers and more from their relative status. The overall response rate for the two areas was 50.5%, with little difference in the interest evoked by the survey in the two areas.

The response rates of the different professionals varied considerably, with most groups ranging from 42% to 70%. High response rates (>75%) were achieved from community psychiatric nurses (CPNs), child and adolescent psychiatrists and occupational therapists (OTs) in mental health services. Low response rates (<5%) were obtained from GPs, nurses on mental health units and wards, and accident and emergency staff. It is probable that these professionals were less likely than other respondents to see the survey subject matter as immediately relevant to their work. Birchall and Hallett's (1995)

Table 8.1: Survey respondents

By profession	Number of respondents	Percentage of total group
Health visitors	67	13
GPs	19	4
Paediatricians	11	2
Accident and emergency staff	4	1
Adult psychiatry staff	58	12
Child and adolescent psychiatrists and psychologists	19	4
Community psychiatric nurses	56	11
Occupational and creative therapists	16	3
Mental health social workers	21	4
Mental health resource centre workers	33	6
Child care social workers	104	21
Child care family centre workers	18	4
Emergency duty team	2	0.5
Police	10	2
Voluntary agency staff – mental health	8	2
Voluntary agency child care	22	4
Children's guardians	15	3
Residential child care workers	7	1
Other	2	0.5
Not answered	8	2
Total	**500**	**100**

survey of key professionals involved in child protection work achieved a similarly low response rate from GPs. Some professional groups included in the sample, such as GPs, were clearly under-represented, while small numbers from other groups, such as OTs and creative therapists, represented a high proportion of the staff in the two areas.

Respondent characteristics

As with most organisations in the fields of health and social care, women predominated among the respondents, constituting 74% of the sample. The vast majority of respondents (86%) were practitioners, with the remainder being middle managers. Generally, the respondent group can be described as an experienced group of practitioners with over 93% having more than two years' experience in health or social care, and nearly two thirds having more than six years' experience. Just under a quarter of respondents had changed their job in the past two years, half had been in their current job for between two and six years, and nearly 15% had been in their present post for between seven and 11 years. While there appeared to be some turnover in the workforces in each research site, there was also a high proportion of experienced staff who had remained in the same jobs for substantial periods of time. Respondents' answers to the survey were analysed in terms of their length of experience, but this did not seem to be significantly associated with any particular responses.

Respondents' experience of families with maternal mental health problems

The level of the respondent group's experience over the past two years with families where there were both maternal mental health problems and childcare concerns appeared high. This was true for both the localities studied. Only

centre workers, or whom just

experience of this sort of work. While the total number of GPs responding to the survey was low, the finding concerning the small number of cases encountered does suggest a lack of experience. This is understandable given the wide span of GPs' responsibilities across the population. It is quite possible that GPs may encounter concerns about child protection where there are also issues of parental mental health problems comparatively infrequently. This becomes particularly evident when GPs' caseloads are compared to the workloads of other professionals; for example, child care social workers, who work with a much smaller and more vulnerable proportion of the population. Other professionals need to take this lack of familiarity with such work into account. The limited experience of mental health resource centre workers may reflect the fact that women with children are less likely to use mental health resource centres, experiencing them as catering predominantly for adults without children. Alternatively, this finding may reflect a focus on the individual service user, that is, the mother rather than the whole family, by resource centre staff.

In attempting to identify which groups were most likely to have high levels of experience in this type of work, it proved difficult to find very substantial differences between professional groups. However, mental health social workers and health visitors were the practitioners who were most likely to have worked with more than 10 such families in the past two years. The distribution of relevant experience across professional groups was very similar across the two study areas.

In addition, the length of time that individuals had spent in their current post did not appear to be particularly influential in determining the overall levels of experience of respondents. While those who identified themselves as managers appeared slightly less likely than practitioners to have worked at all in this field in the past two years, they were also more likely to have worked with a high number of such cases. This was presumably in a supervisory rather than a 'hands-on' capacity, although it may also be a result of practitioners who had moved into management reporting on their previous experience.

In general, the respondents' levels of employment experience did not appear to be a significant factor in determining their responses to the survey questions. Other variables, including gender and whether or not respondents were managers or practitioners, were also examined to discover whether they had any particular bearing on respondents' views. However, no significant associations concerning these factors were found and consequently the discussion of the survey findings will centre on the analysis of the findings by professional group.

Professional roles and remits

A number of commentators have noted the gaps created by organisational divides between children's and adults' services in health and social care (Weir and Douglas, 1999; Reder et al, 2000b). Writers in this field tend to assume that different professional groups focus their attention on particular family members. Such differences in practitioner perspectives are seen to arise from the primary responsibilities of professionals (Weir, 1999).

In order to explore the extent to which different professional groups aligned themselves with parents or children, respondents were asked to indicate whether they saw themselves advocating on behalf of particular family members. Ninety per cent of respondents agreed that they saw it as their task to advocate on behalf of particular family members. The groups who were less likely to see this as a part of their role were the police and GPs. Health visitors and those working in child and adolescent psychiatry were unanimous in their belief that advocating on behalf of a particular family member was part of their role.

Some professionals did see themselves as advocates for one particular grouping within the family. For example, the majority of child care social workers answering this question saw themselves as advocating on behalf of children. On the other hand, GPs were unanimous that they had a responsibility to advocate for all family members. Other professional groups, while indicating a particular focus on children or mothers, also reported advocating on behalf of other family members. As Table 8.2 shows, 85% of health visitors saw it as their task to advocate for all family members, while 76% also considered that it was their task to advocate on behalf of children, and some 69% viewed themselves as advocates for the mother. Those working in adult services, such as mental health social workers, reported a primary focus on mothers, but also considered that they had a role in advocating for all family members. Staff working in adult psychiatry presented a similar picture. However, CPNs presented a somewhat different pattern, with just over a third indicating that they acted as advocates for children, 42% saying that they saw themselves as advocates for the mother and over two thirds describing themselves as advocates for the whole family.

Table 8.2: Family members' needs advocated by professionals[a]

	Mother's	Children's	All family members'
Health visitors	37 (69%)	41 (76%)	46 (85%)
GPs	3 (27%)	3 (27%)	11 (100%)
Paediatricians		2 (25%)	5 (63%)
Adult psychiatry staff	20 (54%)	12 (32%)	20 (54%)
Child and adolescent psychiatrists and psychologists	8 (44%)	14 (78%)	10 (56%)
	18 (42%)	17 (38%)	32 (71%)

Notes:

[a] Practitioners responding to this question were able to choose more than one category of answers.

[b] Some professional groups consisting of small numbers of respondents who answered this question have not been shown as separate entries on this table but are included in the total.

These findings paint a picture of professionals fluctuating in their representation of different family members' needs and shifting their focus between family members at different points in time. It suggests that practitioners cannot always assume that those working in health or adult services will necessarily advocate on behalf of the mother or that those working in child care will inevitably see themselves as representing only the child's interests. The only two professional groups who appeared to be consistent as to whose interests they represented were child care social workers and GPs. This seems explicable given child care social workers' commitment to the principle that the child's needs are paramount in child protection cases and the GP's role as a family practitioner. However, the often inextricable links between the welfare of parents and their children's needs means that child care social workers cannot afford to neglect parents' needs (Stanley and Penhale, 1999; Sheppard, 2002).

The focus group discussions that informed the design of the survey identified risk as a key theme in work with families where mothers had mental health problems. As noted in Chapter Five of this book, the professionals who participated in the focus groups acknowledged the possibility that, at times, risk might be invoked by professionals as a means of accessing services and resources for families. When asked whether they had ever in the past two years over-emphasised the degree of risk in order to access services, 59% of the survey respondents reported that they had never done so. However, as Table 8.3 shows, 38% of respondents said that they had occasionally or sometimes

Table 8.3: Over-emphasising the degree of risk in order to access services (all professional groups)

Risk over-emphasised to access services	Number	%
No	252	60.5
Yes, occasionally	119	29.0
Yes, sometimes	39	9.0
Yes, often	2	0.5
Not answered	5	1.0
Total	**417**[a]	**100.0**

Note: [a] The total number of respondents is less than the overall size of the sample as those without relevant experience did not answer the question.

done so. This may reflect an increasing willingness by professionals to acknowledge the way in which resource shortfalls can impact on risk assessment. The only professionals whose responses differed significantly from this pattern were children's guardians (in site A), of whom 80% reported that they never over-emphasised the degree of risk. In research site B, the professionals whose responses showed a significant difference were those working in adult psychiatry (excluding CPNs), of whom 74% said that they never over-emphasised the degree of risk.

Those respondents who acknowledged that they did, at times, over-emphasise risk were likely to identify these risks as either a risk of significant harm to a child or children or as a risk involving a severe mental health problem. Child care social workers emerged as the one group that was more likely to identify risks to the child than risks involving parental mental health problems. By comparison, the professionals were less inclined to identify risk in terms of a need for registration on the child protection register with only 26.5% of those who acknowledged over-emphasising risk indicating that they had characterised risk in this more formal and procedural way. However, it is worth noting that these respondents were prepared to invoke the child protection registration system specifically as a means of accessing resources.

An increased awareness of the risks posed to children and mothers by domestic violence could be seen in the finding that 11% of those respondents answering this question recorded identifying risks involving domestic violence. This small group included a mixture of professionals, in which health workers predominated, but also included a number of child care social workers. As we saw in Chapter Six of this book, the women interviewed for the study described significant levels of experience of domestic violence.

Communicating with mothers

One of the clear findings delivered by the Department of Health's *Messages from research* was that "the needs of parents and children cannot be compartmentalised" (DoH, 1995a, p 44). Together with the provisions of Part III of the 1989 Children Act, this has provided statutory and voluntary services with a remit to deliver support services to parents. For mothers with mental health problems, the opportunity to discuss their needs with a responsive professional is likely to be the foundation of any effective intervention package. The mothers interviewed in this study considered listening and understanding to be key elements of effective professional intervention (see Chapter Seven of this book). In order to try to establish the extent to which work with families with mental health problems was user-focused, respondents were asked to identify opportunities for active listening in their work. The term 'active listening'

provision of active listening was not appropriate to their role.

As Table 8.4 shows, there were variations between professional groups in respect of opportunities for active listening. In particular, child care social workers were significantly less likely than mental health social workers and CPNs to feel that they were able to undertake this sort of work. This finding confirms the mothers' perceptions that child care social workers generally did not provide the availability and listening skills they valued. Child care social workers' own acknowledgement of their limitations in this area suggests that the mothers' views were not simply a response to the statutory role of child care social workers. Child care social work, particularly those teams dealing with child protection, has experienced staff shortages and an increasing shift to

Table 8.4: Professionals able to offer mothers with mental health problems adequate opportunities for active listening

	All respondents	Child care support workers	Mental health support workers	Community psychiatric nurses
Yes	265 (64%)	34 (38%)	16 (80%)	40 (83%)
No	94 (22%)	38 (43%)	3 (15%)	6 (13%)
No, not appropriate to my role	53 (13%)	14 (16%)	1 (5%)	2 (4%)
N/A	5 (1%)	3 (3%)	–	–
Total	417[a] (100%)	89 (100%)	20 (100%)	48 (100%)

Note: [a] The total number of respondents is less than the overall size of the sample as those without relevant experience did not answer the question.

the care management model of assessment and service brokerage. These factors have combined to restrict child care social workers' opportunities to engage with families on a therapeutic or counselling level. Such findings are relevant when considering which professional group – if any – should take the lead responsibility for working with this group of families with their particular set of complex needs.

NINE

Conceptualising needs and evaluating risk

This chapter explores the ways in which the professionals surveyed in our
~~~~~~~~ ~~~ ~~~~~~~ ~~~~~~ ~~~~~~ ~~~~~~~ ~~~~ We were particularly

Conceptualising needs

The survey asked professionals to list what they considered to be the three
most important needs of mothers with mental health problems. In response,
we received a wide range of answers. These were grouped into four broad
categories (Figure 9.1). Two thirds (276) identified resources to support and
maintain parenting. Such resources included provision of childcare, contact
with absent children, respite care, practical support, financial support and
assistance with parenting skills. For instance, one practitioner described a need
for "practical hands-on help with children". Another suggested:

> "appropriate care for children when experiencing particularly difficult times,
> eg nursery placements, childminders."

A similar proportion (274) identified the mothers' needs for professional
intervention or treatment for their mental health problems. This cluster of
responses was relatively specific and included such answers as "appropriate and
effective medication and treatment" or "professional interventions such as
therapy". The mothers interviewed were less likely to emphasise their need for
formal treatment, although talking therapies were valued. Some of those
interviewed were unhappy about taking drugs and expressed an interest in
coming off their medication.

In the third category of responses, just over half of the professionals indicated
the importance of emotional support for mothers. This support, therefore, was
treated as a separate category, distinct from the more practical forms of support

Figure 9.1: Professionals' perceptions of needs of mothers with mental health problems

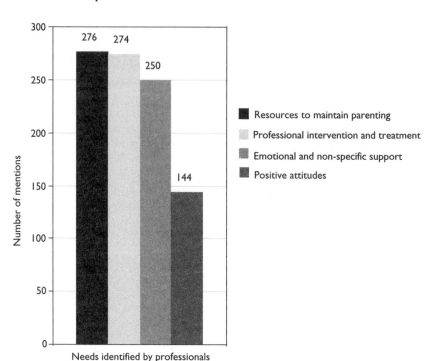

emphasised in the first grouping, although it is necessary to be aware that 'emotional support' covered quite a broad spectrum in terms of the responses given. For example, some practitioners identified a need for "opportunities to talk and someone to listen and believe", without identifying the source of support, while others focused on the role of family and friends in providing emotional sustenance. Some respondents also acknowledged the potential for professionals to assist in this area:

"Input from services who can offer support, help or advice."

As we saw in Chapter Seven of this book, mothers also valued professionals who were able to provide such input.

The fourth and smallest group of answers from the practitioners concerned what were broadly defined as positive attitudes towards mothers. This cluster of responses attracted considerably fewer mentions from participants, with only a third of respondents (144) citing this area as important for mothers. Within this grouping of replies, such elements as non-judgmental approaches, advocacy, information and involvement and support and confidence for women in their role as mothers were included:

"Not to be stigmatised as unable to fulfil mothering role."

"Need to be included in what is going on (partnership) and need to be respected and kept informed."

Again, this finding becomes particularly salient when the mothers' own views concerning what constituted the most relevant and helpful type of professional responses are considered.

As we saw earlier, one of the key factors to emerge from the women's evaluations of professionals was the value accorded to practitioners who were

mindset that views the mother principally in terms of the risk she may pose to her child. This mismatch between the perceptions of service users and professionals concerning the core elements of their transactions is not a new phenomenon and has been well documented – but the issue still needs to be addressed. A focus on risk which is reinforced by practitioners' awareness of the 'blame culture' (see Chapter Five of this book for discussion of this theme in the focus groups) may make it difficult for practitioners to sustain positive, non-judgmental attitudes. The following section describes and compares practitioners' approaches to evaluating risk.

Evaluating risk

As we saw in Chapter Six of this book, a significant proportion of professionals surveyed reported that they had over-emphasised risk, at least occasionally, in order to access services on behalf of families they worked with. The assessment of risk was explored in more depth by including a series of 12 short vignettes in the questionnaire.

Vignettes involving hypothetical situations have been used with some success in survey research to try to identify, and even measure, differences in responses to specific scenarios (Finch, 1984). For instance, Hetherington et al (2001) explored the responses of groups of child care and mental health professionals from 13 countries to a vignette describing a family where the mother had mental illness. Their study found that child care professionals tended to underestimate the seriousness of the mother's illness. Furthermore, they identified a need for teaching on mental health for child care social workers. Work by Birchall and Hallett (1995) developed the use of vignettes within child protection research. Their research, building on earlier studies by Giovannoni and Becerra (1979) and Fox and Dingwell (1985), provided a model for the successful use of scenarios in order to assess the variations in professional assessments of the severity of child abuse.

Some commentators have suggested that focus groups, with their facility for generating stories and anecdotes, are a useful source of the raw materials for development of scenarios or vignettes of especial relevance for the group being studied (Barbour, 1999; Bloor et al, 2001). As described in Chapter Five, we employed such an approach in this study and were able to use some of the discussion generated in the three interprofessional focus groups held in Stage One of the research to inform the design of the vignettes.

Following the focus group stage of the research, a series of 12 short vignettes, where the mothers had mental health problems and there were child protection issues, was developed. These were included in the questionnaire as a separate section (Table 9.1). Survey respondents were asked to use a nine-point scale to rate each of these vignettes in terms of the severity of the risks to the children described. These vignettes painted brief pictures of families in which the mothers had varying mental health problems and received various amounts of support, and in which the children were experiencing different levels and types of abuse. While some of the vignettes specified the impact of the abuse on the child or children, others left this question open. In addition to the input from the focus groups, the development of the vignettes was informed by consultation with a range of professionals and service user representatives. Advice concerning the construction of the vignettes was also sought from the research advisory groups in each of the study locations.

Analysis of the vignettes involved summarising and comparing respondents' ratings of both individual vignettes and of the whole series. The overall mean scores for the individual vignettes were calculated and compared using the One-Sample T-test to determine whether differences in scores were significant. The mean scores of different occupational groups were also examined; ANOVA testing was used to establish statistical significance. In an attempt to gain further clarity, occupational groups related to each other within a wider category (for example, 'general medical professionals' or 'psychiatric medical professionals') were also compared.

The respondents' scores for the individual vignettes indicated that they were able to discriminate between different situations and levels of risk, with some vignettes attracting higher mean scores than others. For example, Vignette 12 elicited the highest mean score from respondents and Vignette 8 achieved the lowest. In order to determine which factors had most influence on the respondents' ratings, the vignettes were classified along four different dimensions:

- diagnosis;
- type of abuse;
- level of support;
- severity of impact on the child or children.

Table 9.1: The vignettes

1. A mother who suffers from postnatal depression has difficulty in getting up in the mornings and in managing the home. She has three children, aged six, four and 10 months. Her mother sometimes helps out.
2. A mother with schizophrenia experiences periods when she is distressed by delusions in which she believes that her two children, aged six and four, are suffering from cancer and will shortly die. Her husband constantly attempts to reassure her.
3. A divorced mother with an obsessive-compulsive disorder is constantly [illegible] wash their hands and faces. The children have sore, red [illegible]

[illegible] their father's flat nearby.

6. A single mother with a severe depressive disorder believes that she is 'a bad mother'. She repeatedly asks her five-year-old to reassure her about her mothering.
7. A single mother with a personality disorder is excessively critical of her two children, aged seven and four. They are both aggressive with other children.
8. A mother with a history of self-harm receives support from a mental health worker. When she finds herself becoming distressed, she usually seeks appropriate support. Her children, aged 14, 11 and nine, worry about her.
9. A mother with a personality disorder and alcohol problem finds it hard to keep appointments and to provide regular meals. Her only child, aged 10, does much of the shopping and takes his mother to out-patient appointments at the hospital. The family receives considerable support from neighbours.
10. A mother with schizophrenia will only feed her four-year-old tinned food as she believes that all fresh food is contaminated by pesticides. Her partner does not intervene in her care of the child.
11. A mother with recurrent periods of depression finds it hard to prevent her 13-year-old daughter staying out late at night. The daughter has become involved in sexual activity and drug taking with older children. Her stepfather attempts to support his wife.
12. A mother with a personality disorder has difficulty in controlling her two children, aged seven and five. She regularly slaps and kicks them, sometimes leaving bruises.

The mean scores were calculated and compared for the different vignettes within each grouping. This allowed the research team to identify which of these dimensions was most influential on the decisions made by respondents. In this context, significance was seen to reside in a difference of at least two points on the scale. Using this criterion, only one of the four dimensions appeared to be relevant in determining professionals' ratings of the vignettes: *severity of the impact of abuse on the child*. The harm experienced by children appeared to be more significant, therefore, in shaping professional judgment than other variables, such as diagnosis or type of abuse. Variations in levels of support had some impact on ratings but the distance between the mean scores for the low support vignettes and for those depicting high support was less than the two points required for significance.

The extent of variation between professional groups in their ratings of the vignettes was not great. However, a comparison of mean scores for occupational groups across all 12 vignettes showed that GPs, health visitors and child and adolescent psychiatrists produced the highest mean scores. Although judgments made on vignettes cannot be assumed to be reproduced in real-life situations, the health professionals who consistently assessed the perceived risks to children within the scenarios higher than other professionals might be more ready in practice to identify risks for children in families where mothers had mental health problems.

Additionally, those practitioners working in child care services in non-health settings had lower mean scores across all the vignettes. This indicates a reduced threshold for risk among child care staff in social care, a finding that receives some support from Birchall and Hallett's (1995) study, which showed that child care social workers produced the lowest ratings of abuse and that health visitors gave the highest, indicating significant divergence between the two groups. It is not surprising that those practitioners for whom child abuse is a regular and central component of their workload should have higher thresholds for identifying risk than those who encounter significant harm less frequently. Practitioners not used to working with child abuse are more likely to rate risks as exceptional and severe. Mothers may find that healthcare professionals such as health visitors and those working in child and adolescent psychiatry may, despite their expressed interest in the wider family noted in Chapter Eight, be inclined to emphasise risks of significant harm for children.

There was one vignette in the series (Table 9.1, vignette 10) which, despite being designed to illustrate a potentially major risk for a child, was allocated low risk scores by respondents from all professional backgrounds. This vignette involved the implication and inclusion of the child within a mother's delusional system. As noted in Chapter One of this book, there is a degree of consensus among researchers that such delusions can indicate a high level of risk for the child (Cassell and Coleman, 1995; Falkov, 1998). Therefore, respondents' lack of awareness of such risks is a cause for concern. The risks described in the vignettes were potential rather than actual, and this may have influenced respondents' ratings. However, the professionals' rating of this vignette does lend support to Hetherington et al's (2001) recommendation that practitioners require further training to develop their knowledge of mental health issues.

The other key mental health issue addressed by the vignettes was the responses evoked by the diagnosis of personality disorder. Following the discussions concerning this diagnosis in the focus group stage of the research, a number of the vignettes were designed to include mothers with a personality disorder. The use of this diagnosis within psychiatry has been increasingly recognised as contentious; indeed, proposals for the detention of individuals with personality disorder contained in the draft Mental Health Bill have been extremely controversial (DoH, 2002b).

...lity disorder ranges over a number of key

(Dolan and Coid, 1993), with variations in defining the condition making evaluations of intervention particularly difficult.

In the pilot study (described in Chapter Four of this book), we found a number of examples of the term being used to describe the mental health difficulties that mothers experienced. The focus group discussions produced widespread agreement about the imprecise use of the term 'personality disorder' and its function as a label that could exclude women from services. While diagnosis was not the key variable influencing practitioners' risk assessments across the full set of vignettes, personality disorder was found to consistently attract higher ratings when the practitioners' ratings of the different diagnoses used in the vignettes were compared. This was true of all professional groups, with the exception of GPs and paediatricians, who were inclined to rate schizophrenia slightly higher. This suggests that the practitioners in our study had absorbed the confusing and predominantly negative messages associated with the diagnosis of personality disorder. Mothers who are described as having personality disorders may be particularly likely to attract judgmental attitudes from practitioners.

The interviews with mothers showed them detecting and responding to such negative attitudes. For mothers labelled with personality disorders, a reluctance to access and use services may be further intensified by practitioners' responses to their diagnosis. These mothers may wait for a full-blown crisis to occur before seeking assistance. The pessimism associated with a diagnosis of personality disorder can, in this way, become a self-fulfilling prophecy.

Training needs

Variations in conceptions of need between professionals and service users, as well as suggestions that risk assessments are based on gaps in knowledge or negative attitudes concerning mental health problems, indicate a need for further training. Such training might introduce professionals to service users' perspectives and evaluations of services and develop their awareness of the knowledge and values that they bring to the assessment of risk (Stanley and Manthorpe, 1997). A number of survey respondents commented on the need for joint training in this area, and interprofessional training on work with families where parents have mental health problems is widely recommended (Falkov, 1998; Bernard and Douglas, 1999; Reder and Duncan, 1999).

Research by Murrell (1999) in Kent in the late 1990s found that there was a clear need for joint training to underpin collaboration and joint working. Only half of the respondents considered that the existing arrangements for child care and mental health practitioners to work together were satisfactory. Further, only 15% of practitioners had received any post-qualifying training in mental health and the possible effects on parenting. Within mental health and child care services, there was a lack of understanding, knowledge and clarity about respective roles and responsibilities. Joint training was perceived as a key means of resolving such difficulties. When asked what types of training were needed to improve practice, practitioners from both child care and mental health indicated a keen interest in looking at the effects of mental illness on children. A need for specialist staff in both types of provision, who had received joint training, was also identified.

Hetherington et al's study (2001) also emphasised problems in communication and trust between service users and professionals, and identified variations concerning appropriate levels of shared professional knowledge and information between practitioners from different disciplines. The study found gaps in professionals' knowledge and a lack of understanding concerning the roles and expertise of different practitioners. The final report of their European project recommended that the knowledge base concerning mental health, child development (including child protection) and social structures should be extended to a wider group of professionals. In addition, knowledge and understanding of the role and function of other agencies, in particular at local levels, should be broadened. As their report states:

> We recommend that urgent attention is given to the increase at the pre-qualifying level in education on mental health for child welfare professionals (particularly social workers), and on child development and family support for professionals in adult psychiatry. At post-qualifying level, shared training on local services and on the development of particular skills is needed to develop both the knowledge of the functioning of other agencies and the confidence that depends on that knowledge. (Hetherington et al, 1999, p 103)

There is some evidence that such programmes are being designed and delivered. Pearce (2003) has described the development of multi-agency training in work with children, families and mental health needs. The course consists of a two-day programme and has been specifically planned to:

> offer participants the opportunity to look over the wall into the mysterious workings of other services and to see how a constructive dialogue between workers from different services could enhance the provision of services to families. (Pearce, 2003, p 115)

wide range of professionals are included among the aims to expand practitioners' knowledge base in relation to both mental health and child protection, and has also included sessions covering relevant legislation in both areas.

The training uses a developing case study as the focus for learning. Participants have worked together in interprofessional groups to identify relevant knowledge and approaches for assessment, planning, crisis intervention and longer-term interventions. Mothers' perspectives and views have been introduced to participants and issues concerning interprofessional work have also been explored. The training has been positively evaluated and anecdotal evidence from practitioners suggests that it has contributed to improved confidence in practice, particularly relating to knowledge and understanding and increased willingness to work collaboratively in this area.

However, the professional groups invited to attend such training have expressed varying levels of interest and commitment. In common with other such training events (Weir et al, 1997), uptake has been low among psychiatrists and medical practitioners. This reflects different work patterns, organisational structures and variations in the extent to which interprofessional training is perceived as relevant. Responses to calls for training are likely to reflect established patterns of interprofessional communication and coordination. The survey findings on these key issues are explored in Chapter Ten.

Interprofessional communication and coordination

with GPs, while 27% reported the same frequency of problems with adult psychiatrists. These rates were substantially higher than the levels of difficulties identified for other professional groups. For example, only 17% reported consistent or frequent difficulties in working with child care social workers, and 12% had a similar level of problems with community psychiatric nurses (CPNs).

The professionals with whom respondents were least likely to experience difficulties were health visitors: 58% reported that they hardly ever or never had problems in coordinating work. Lupton et al (2001) report similar levels of satisfaction from other professionals commenting on their work with health visitors. The other groups of practitioners with whom respondents appeared to have fewer problems were child and family centre workers (49% reported hardly ever or never having difficulties) and child care social workers (42% reported hardly ever or never having difficulties).

Child care social workers, child and family centre workers and children's guardians (formerly known as Guardians ad Litem, this group of professionals will all have trained and practised as child care social workers) were the professional groups most likely to report frequent or constant difficulties with GPs. Over half of the respondents in these three professional groups described a high level of difficulties. In contrast, GPs did not identify similar difficulties in relation to these groups. Few health visitors and CPNs reported high levels of problems with GPs. The professionals who themselves worked in primary care settings, such as health visitors and GPs, were most likely to report very seldom having difficulties in coordinating work with GPs. About half of CPNs sometimes had difficulties with GPs. Professionals working in adult psychiatry were also likely to report that they sometimes had difficulties.

Table 10.1: Difficulties in coordinating work with other professional groups (all respondents) (%)

Professional group	Always/ frequently	Sometimes	Hardly ever/ never	Not answered
Health visitors	6	25	58	11
GPs	35	37	22	7
Paediatricians	13	27	34	27
Accident and emergency staff	11	25	37	28
Adult psychiatrists	27	32	22	19
Child and adolescent psychiatrists	15	26	35	24
Ward nurses	11	30	34	26
Adult psychologists	15	27	28	30
Child and adolescent psychologists	10	20	42	29
Community psychiatric nurses	12	30	41	17
Mental health social workers	12	26	38	24
Mental health resource centre workers	6	20	39	36
Child care social workers	17	25	42	17
Child care family centre workers	7	19	49	25
Emergency duty team	8	19	40	40
Police	8	23	40	30
Voluntary agency mental health	6	23	30	40
Voluntary agency child care	5	20	36	39
Teachers	12	27	32	29

The child care social workers' evaluations of work with GPs are consonant with the findings of both Hallett's (1995) research and Lupton et al's (2001) study. Both identified high levels of dissatisfaction with GPs' performance in child protection work and found that child care social workers expressed particular concerns about GPs' poor rates of attendance at child protection case conferences. Lupton et al (2001) found that health visitors were also quite critical of GPs' performance in child protection work. However, the question posed in our study was less concerned with evaluating other professionals' performance in a particular sphere of work and more with an assessment of the problems of coordinating work with a particular professional group.

Again it was child care social workers (43%) and child care family centre workers (50%) who most often identified frequent or constant difficulties in working with adult psychiatrists. Interestingly, those working in adult psychiatry were more likely than other professionals to describe high levels of problems in coordinating their work with child care social workers. In contrast, 45% of mental health social workers said that they hardly ever or never had difficulties with adult psychiatrists. This rate compared favourably with the 28% of CPNs who hardly ever or never had difficulties, but the number of mental health social workers responding to this question was small. The Royal College of Psychiatrists' (2002) guidelines on working with families stress the need for psychiatrists to be familiar with national guidance on interprofessional collaboration and local child protection procedures. Members of the college are urged to develop their awareness of local support services for families and forge links with staff in local services. However, no advice is given on what

workers. Likewise, community mental health workers reported few problems in coordinating work with child care social workers and child care resource centre workers.

Interprofessional problems with confidentiality

The *Working together* guidelines (DoH et al, 1999) acknowledge that professional practices concerning confidentiality can establish barriers to effective communication and collaboration. Codes of confidentiality differ, as can the criteria used by professional groups for breaching confidentiality, despite the published guidance. Health visitors were the group with which practitioners were most likely to experience very few problems of confidentiality: just under two thirds of all respondents said they hardly ever or never had problems of confidentiality with this group. However, as Table 10.2 shows, there was also a considerable degree of satisfaction in this respect with child care social workers, family centre workers and with mental health social workers.

Again, the two professional groups most likely to attract negative ratings with regard to their practice on confidentiality were adult psychiatrists and GPs. Almost a third of respondents reported always or frequently having problems of confidentiality with GPs, and nearly a quarter of respondents described always having a high level of problems with adult psychiatrists. A breakdown of these responses by professional group produced findings similar to those achieved on the question of coordinating services. That is, child care social workers, children's guardians and voluntary sector child care workers were most likely to cite problems with GPs, while difficulties with confidentiality in relation to adult psychiatrists were most likely to be identified as frequent by

Table 10.2: Frequency of confidentiality problems with other professionals (all respondents) (%)

Professional group	Always/ frequently	Sometimes	Hardly ever/ never	Not answered
Health visitors	5	15	61	19
GPs	28	24	33	15
Paediatricians	6	13	38	43
Accident and emergency staff	6	12	37	45
Adult psychiatrists	22	22	30	27
Child and adolescent psychiatrists	14	21	34	31
Ward nurses	8	18	30	34
Adult psychologists	18	23	26	34
Child and adolescent psychologists	13	21	32	34
Community psychiatric nurses	12	27	35	26
Mental health social workers	7	21	40	32
Mental health resource centre workers	5	14	20	51
Child care social workers	6	16	52	26
Child care family centre workers	3	10	42	45
Emergency duty team	4	8	50	38
Police	7	19	42	34
Voluntary agency mental health	8	17	23	53
Voluntary agency child care	4	16	28	52
Teachers	7	21	35	37

health visitors, child care social workers and voluntary sector child care workers. Lupton et al (2001, p 161) found that non-health colleagues "tended not to be too empathic" with medical practitioners' concerns about confidentiality. However, it is worth noting that, in our study, health visitors were also likely to identify high levels of problems pertaining to confidentiality in their work with adult psychiatrists. Rouse (2002) notes that health visitors can experience dilemmas of confidentiality when they are given access to information by a medical clinician who is not willing for this information to be shared with other professionals.

Confidentiality has been identified as a barrier to professional communication and coordination in a range of mental health inquiry reports (Ritchie et al, 1994; Blom-Cooper et al, 1996; Wood et al, 1996). Fulford (2001) describes professionals in mental health services as experiencing a paradox of confidentiality with pressures to share information with other professionals (usually justified by the need to assess and manage risk) conflicting with the increasing emphasis on an individual's privacy. Bollas (2001) goes further in arguing that therapeutic relationships with patients cannot be sustained in the face of current pressures for information sharing. Families where the vulnerabilities of one family member may render another family member vulnerable present practitioners with particular challenges of confidentiality. Trowell (2001) stresses the need for GPs working with more than one member of a family to receive training on confidentiality in issues of child abuse, while Harbour (2001) recommends that guidelines on confidentiality be developed for adult psychiatrists treating patients where there are child protection issues.

Our findings on problems with confidentiality are similar to those concerning

perceptions of them as causing few problems in the area of confidentiality. Possession of specialised knowledge and a lack of willingness to share it are intimately connected with high professional status and its wide recognition.

Taking a lead in risk assessment

Respondents were asked to identify which professional group they considered best able to assess risks of significant harm to children where mothers had mental health problems. Only three groups attracted any significant support:

- 22% of all respondents identified child care social workers as the group best able to assess the risk of significant harm;
- 19% indicated that whoever was most involved with the family was best able to perform this task;
- 13% chose health visitors.

Each of the remaining professional groups attracted less than 10% of respondents' nominations, with the majority of groups receiving only a few expressions of support.

Some distinct differences emerged from exploring who was most likely to nominate particular groups. Child care social workers received the highest number of mentions from child care social workers themselves (36%). However, they also received high numbers of nominations from CPNs (23%) and those working in adult psychiatry (23%). The professional groups most likely to consider that this task was best undertaken by the professional with most family involvement were, interestingly, those groups most clearly located on the interface between mental health services and family services. These included mental health social workers (30%) and child and adolescent psychiatrists and psychologists (32%). CPNs and mental health resource centre workers, who may have some involvement with the family, but whose perspective is more focused on the adult mental health service user, were fairly evenly divided between nominating child care social workers and whoever had the most family involvement.

The groups most likely to nominate health visitors for this task were health visitors themselves (42%) and GPs (77%). No other groups favoured health visitors for this task over child care social workers or whoever was most involved. This pattern of responses seems to confine the support for a key role for health visitors in risk assessment to the primary care setting.

Some distinct differences can be discerned, therefore, between professional groups in their perceptions of who was best able to assess the risk of significant harm to children. While there was overall support for child care workers to undertake this function, those groups with a foot in each camp of adult mental health care and family services support the claims of the worker with most family involvement, so retaining the possibility that they themselves could assume this role. Meanwhile, health visitors and GPs were more likely to see the necessary skills as located in their own primary care setting. Similar response patterns were found when the question of which professional group should assume a lead role was addressed.

Identifying a lead service

Overall, there was substantial support for designating one professional group as the lead or coordinating service, with nearly three-quarters of respondents supporting this suggestion. Those respondents who replied positively were then asked to indicate which professional group they would nominate for such a role. The group to attract the greatest number of nominations (37%) were the child care social workers, with their highest levels of support coming from their own ranks. As Table 10.3 shows, 64% of child care social workers answering this question nominated their own profession. Similarly, nearly all the children's guardians nominated child care social workers for a lead role. The only professional group to nominate health visitors over and above all other groups were GPs. Those working in adult psychiatry and CPNs were slightly more likely to propose mental health social workers for this lead role than they were to nominate child care social workers, although child care social workers were also nominated by both these groups. Mental health social workers themselves, along with psychiatrists and psychologists working in child and adolescent services, and mental health resource centre workers were most likely to opt for whichever professional was most involved with the family.

While child care social workers clearly emerged from our respondent group as the favourites for assuming a lead role, as we have seen, much of their support derived from their own ranks. Among other professional groups, there

**Table 10.3: Professional groups most frequently nominated for lead/
coordinating role by respondent groups**

| Respondent group | Nominees for lead/coordinating role | | | | |
	Health visitors	Community psychiatric nurses	Mental health social workers	Child care social workers	People most involved[a]
Health visitors	23	13	6	31	17
	75	–	–	8	–
			ˀ꜀	22	11
Childrens guaꞇ ꞇꞇ...					
All respondents	10	ꜱ	. .		

Notes:

[a] This category refers to the practitioner with most involvement with the family, regardless of their professional background.

The figures in the horizontal columns do not add up to 100 as some respondents nominated other professional groups. Only those professional groups nominated by significant numbers are shown here.

was some interest in assigning this role to mental health social workers or to the people or person most involved with a family. However, even when child care social workers were excluded from the respondent group for the purposes of analysis, they still emerged as the favoured group for the lead role, although the proportion nominating them dropped from 37% to 27%.

Among the professionals, there was acknowledgement of child care social workers' competence in assessing significant harm. There was also some general enthusiasm for assigning a lead role in working with these families to child care social workers. However, it seemed that practitioners' views on this issue were crosscut by sectional and tribal interests (Dalley, 1989). It was notable that those workers located on the boundary between health and social care appeared more ready to allocate a lead role to whoever was most involved with the family. The majority of health practitioners were unlikely to nominate their own profession for a lead role, whereas social workers, particularly child care social workers, enthusiastically claimed lead status for themselves.

However, it was also evident from the survey that the lines of interprofessional coordination were weakest between child care social workers and both GPs and adult psychiatrists. There is a substantial amount of evidence for GPs' low levels of engagement with child protection (Hallett, 1995; Lupton et al, 2001). In this study, as we saw in Chapter Six of this book, GPs constituted the professional group with the lowest levels of experience of families with parental mental health problems and child care concerns. This lack of experience may make the cases they do encounter extremely challenging, particularly given their definition of their remit to advocate on behalf of all family members. The findings on the difficulties in coordinating work with GPs are of particular concern in view of GPs' responsibilities for treating the majority of those with mental health problems in the community and their role as the gateway to specialist mental health services. Those working in child care services may experience them as impeding attempts to access mental health care for mothers. While care needs to be taken in interpreting the survey data, particularly given the overall low response rate achieved from GPs within our study, these findings question Reder et al's (2000c) suggestion that GPs are ideally placed to bridge the gap between children's and adult's mental health services.

Poor communication with adult psychiatrists will be particularly problematic when mothers experience mental health problems and are heavily involved with psychiatric services. Some of these difficulties can be attributed to differences in knowledge base, training and patterns of service delivery. Sheppard and Kelly's (2001) study of social work intervention with depressed mothers found that social workers and mental health workers conceptualised the women's needs differently, drawing on separate discourses. Issues of professional status and power are also relevant (Lupton et al, 2001; Reder et al, 2000b). The client group focus of the three professions differs, and GPs and child care social workers were the two professional groups demonstrating most intra-group consistency in identifying one part of the family as their primary client.

Other writers (Göpfert et al, 1996; Reder and Duncan, 1999) have used examples from clinical practice to illustrate the difficulties which those working in adult mental health services may experience in acknowledging the presence and needs of children in a family when a parent has mental health problems. We have argued elsewhere (Barbour et al, 2002) that social workers have a good deal of ambivalence about the value of diagnosis and the predominance of the medical model within mental health services. The combination of a distrust of the medical model and a desire for the certainty and predictability that diagnosis is thought to confer can lead to unrealistic and conflicting expectations of adult psychiatry from child care workers.

Reder and Duncan (1999) argue that the safety of the child is not determined by the psychiatric diagnosis of the parent, and that parallel assessments of the parent's psychiatric state and the child's needs are required. We suggest that the assessment of the parent's psychiatric state should contribute to the assessment of parenting capacity but should not be seen as commensurate with such an assessment. Parenting capacity is most appropriately assessed by professionals working in children's services. Child care practitioners need to develop the confidence to use mental health assessments produced by adult psychiatry to inform their own assessments of parenting capacity.

Falkov (1998) notes the lack of established models of joint provision to meet the needs of families where parents have mental health problems. However, some structures are beginning to emerge at the local level. For example, in our study site A, community mental health workers were being attached to family resource centres. Lindsay et al (1999) describe the establishment of local 'consultants' who offer advice to staff in child care and mental health services. Families where parental mental health problems and child protection concerns coexist need support for parents as well as monitoring of children's welfare. This is not to characterise mental health services as lacking a coercive element or children's services as failing to offer families supportive services. However, this dichotomy does also reflect the differential views of services held by the mothers and explored in Chapter Seven of this book. The study findings

ELEVEN

Identifying appropriate resources

The availability of appropriate resources will be a key factor in developing an effective response to families' needs. In mental health services, staff time and ~~'ill~~ ~~are essential~~ components of the service but are often in short supply

~~...what constitutes~~

and domiciliary services, ~~which aim to~~
practical tasks as well as develop users' skills. There are few examples of services that are focused directly on parents with mental health needs. Where such services do exist, they are likely to be provided by the voluntary sector. The New Parent Information Network (NEWPIN), a voluntary organisation which provides support for parents with mental health needs (Cox et al, 1991; Cox, 1993), is probably the best-known example of such a service in the UK, but none of the research sites in this study could boast such a resource. Since mental health needs fluctuate over time, services need to be speedily accessed when they are needed, with the possibility that they can be withdrawn or reduced in intensity when levels of mental health need subside.

Practitioner time is an equally important resource in child care services; Chapter Eight of this book reported the difficulties experienced by child care social workers in offering mothers adequate opportunities for 'active listening'. Other relevant resources include those focused on strengthening or reinforcing parenting skills: these might include support groups for parents and voluntary sector services such as Home Start. The provision of good-quality childcare is a key but rationed service that is much valued by families (Statham et al, 2001). Likewise, respite care for children at times of family crisis or illness can be a key factor in keeping families intact. Such care can take a range of forms with the traditional 'short breaks' provided by foster carers increasingly being augmented by 'support care' or respite fostering arrangements. These allow children to regularly receive part of their care in foster settings, often in the form of after-school or weekend substitute care, particularly at times of stress for families (Winchester, 2003).

Specialist therapies or counselling for children and for the whole family tend to be in short supply, as evidenced by the concerns documented regarding the availability of CAMHS services (Audit Commission, 1999; Mental Health Foundation, 1999; SSI, 2002). Individual therapy may be particularly crucial for children who have experienced abuse. Relevant therapeutic or counselling services for children are also provided in some areas by the voluntary sector and youth services may be involved in providing supportive groups or drop-in facilities for young people. Young carers' groups, which are likely to be provided by the voluntary sector, have proved an effective form of group support for children and young people from families where there is long-term parental illness (Becker et al, 1998).

Messages from research (DoH, 1995a) emphasised the tendency of all services to focus resources on the assessment of risks for children and to then withdraw, leaving families with little in the way of long-term support services. Following this report, the range of supportive services for families has been substantially increased, although their availability across England and Wales is variable and they have developed at different rates in different authorities (Colton et al, 1995; Henricson et al, 2001). In this study, it was notable that practitioners in research site B, where family support services were less well developed, tended to highlight the shortfall in those services, while the respondents in site A were more emphatic about the inaccessibility of mental health services.

Evaluating the accessibility of existing resources

Our study aimed to establish how accessible and relevant existing resources in the two research areas were for families where mothers had mental health problems. Mental health services have been slow to recognise that their users may also be parents (Göpfert et al, 1996; Falkov and Davies, 1997), and many services have been designed for use by single people. Similarly, services aimed at supporting families might lack the specialist skills and flexibility to respond to the particular needs of mothers with mental health problems.

Forty-two per cent of the professionals responding to the survey agreed that there were relevant resources that mothers with mental health problems in their area had difficulty in accessing but which would be valuable for them. Just over a third of respondents did not feel that this was the case. The proportions were very similar in each study site. Table 11.1 identifies the inaccessible resources most frequently cited as community psychiatric nurses (CPNs) and community mental health teams (CMHTs) and family support services, including home helps and Home-Start, and shows the differences in the perceptions of resource availability between the two study sites.

Community mental health services were criticised by the survey respondents, particularly those in site A, for their lack of flexibility and accessibility. Practitioners noted that mothers with mental health problems often did not meet the tightly drawn criteria for receiving mental health services:

Table 11.1: Local resources considered inaccessible for mothers with mental health problems

	Number of times cited		
	Site A[a]	Site B[b]	Total
CPNs/community mental health team	40	13	53
Family support/home help/Home-Start	22	17	39
Childcare/nurseries	12	23	35
...drop-ins	23	12	35
		6	28
Child and adolescent services			
Services for mothers with personality disorder	8	–	

Notes: [a] 130 respondents identified inaccessible resources in Site A.

[b] 79 respondents identified inaccessible resources in Site B.

> "Adult CMHTs only have resources to support severe and enduring mental illness group – this excludes mothers with neurotic disorders, personality disorders or drug/alcohol problems. It is this group who require support and who without support are more damaging to children."

> "There is a community mental health team in my locality but it is often not easy to get them to accept referrals from mothers with ongoing depression...."

The mothers themselves also reported difficulties in accessing CPN services and were aware of their own lack of priority (see Chapters Six and Seven of this book for a full account of their views). One woman reported:

> "I got refused a CPN – I think it's on the grounds that I'm not mentally backward, that's what I believe. Sometimes I think if you can cook and clean and keep a nice house and you can speak a full sentence, that's it, that's the way they look at it."

Sheppard and Kelly's (2001) study also found that mothers with depression frequently failed to meet the eligibility criteria for mental health services. In Chapter Eight of this book, the extent to which practitioners were likely to over-emphasise risks in order to access services was identified. When services are heavily rationed and eligibility criteria are set at a high level, there will be significant temptations for practitioners to represent risks as great. The consequences of such approaches may be severe for families, with an over-emphasis on mental health risks resulting in high levels of medication, hospitalisation and the ensuing stigma, while over-representation of child care risks can entail children being admitted to the looked-after system.

Practitioners recognised that waiting lists could be seen as a disincentive for those mothers who were eligible to receive mental health services:

> "Actual home visits from CPNs seem not to be the norm. Also often a wait of a few weeks to be seen after referral."

While existing family support services were seen to be doing a good job, respondents in both areas felt that such resources needed to be extended and made more accessible:

> "The family support team is very good but nowhere near enough to start to tackle the problems."

> "Family resource centres can provide support to individuals and family members where mental health is an issue. However, clients cannot self refer and there are long waiting lists."

Practitioners saw accessible childcare as a key service for families where mothers had mental health problems. Practitioners, particularly those in research site B, called for "easier access to childminders and additional nursery places". Without childcare, mothers will be unable to access those experiences, such as employment or education, that can boost resilience and self-esteem. Respondents also noted that childcare facilities were necessary for mothers to access mental health provision:

> "We have psychologists and mental health workers, but if the mother cannot access childcare she doesn't benefit from attendance."

> "The mental health resource centre has no crèche facilities."

Respite care from specialist workers was also seen as a potentially valuable resource for families where mothers had mental health problems, especially "respite carers with knowledge of mental health issues for children and families". The mothers' experiences of liaison and communication difficulties with carers (reported in Chapter Seven of this book) reinforce the argument for foster carers and residential child care staff to develop specialist skills and knowledge in working with families where there are parental mental health needs.

Practitioners also commented on the lack of available supported accommodation for the whole family. This issue was also identified by one of the mothers interviewed:

"Well, usually with services it's like, are you ill? If you need to go anywhere they'll get my daughter looked after and I think we come as a package: why don't they ever come up with anything for you together? It's always take one away, look after the other one."

In singling out self-help groups and drop-in centres as resources that could be more accessible for this group of service users, respondents emphasised the need for information concerning such groups to be more widely available and for groups explicitly to target mothers with mental health needs:

find out

women who have expe
women, *The NHS Plan* (DoH, 2000a) proposed that
day services should be available in every health authority by 2004. The consultation document, *Women's mental health: Into the mainstream* (DoH, 2002a), noted that, currently, such resources are provided only by the voluntary sector. The document included an outline service specification for women-only community day services that identified crèche or childcare facilities as a key design principle of such a service (DoH, 2002a, p 54).

The survey respondents also identified counselling services as a resource that needed to be more readily available:

"Many women are referred to this agency who have disclosed sexual abuse. Their current mental health problems are highly likely to be linked to this unresolved form of trauma. There are very few services on offer that can undertake free/long-term work that do not have very long waiting lists."

"Mothers with behavioural problems associated with abusive experiences in their own past are often not considered a priority for counselling, especially if the children are removed and are not likely to return."

The significance attributed by practitioners to the contribution of abusive early experiences to mental health problems in adult life was confirmed by the interviews with mothers (see Chapter Six of this book).

Where resources were available that focused on parents with mental health needs, they were clearly valued and practitioners were keen to see such specialised resources extended. Practitioners from research site B expressed regrets that an in-patient mother and baby unit was no longer available within the immediate area:

"There's a mother and baby unit six miles away but here you have to go to a city mental health facility with no mother and baby specialist nurse or unit."

There were also calls for the local mother and baby CPN service to be developed further:

"There is currently a mother and baby team for mothers who are suffering from mental health problems. However, this team only deals with mothers whose children are up to 18 months...."

There was no discernible relationship between the respondents' professions and the resources they identified as inaccessible. While the practitioners clearly considered that there were relevant resources in their areas which could be made more accessible for families where mothers had mental health problems, mothers were regarded as accorded a low priority within mental health services. Resources aimed at supporting families were in short supply and lacked a sufficient focus on parents with mental health needs.

Valuable resources not available locally

Respondents were also asked to identify resources that would benefit families with maternal mental health problems but were currently unavailable in their local area: these are shown in Table 11.2. While a proportion of respondents did not provide an answer to this question, the resource most frequently identified by those who did was support groups, mother and toddler groups or women's centres:

"Small groups in supportive atmosphere where mothers can benefit from mutual support and access services and advice."

The essence of such groups seemed to be their emphasis on self-help and their location within local communities. In some cases, practitioners specified that these groups should aim to meet particular needs:

"Dedicated self-help groups for (a) mothers with mental health problems who are placed under additional stress by child protection machinery, and (b) mothers who have lost their children through the child protection process."

Drop-in services and community centres also received a significant number of mentions. Again, respondents highlighted the need for such groups to be designed with the needs of mothers and families in mind:

"Drop-in mental health clinics for depressed mothers in particular."

"Locality-based, family-based, drop-in centres."

Practitioners, particularly those in site A, emphasised the importance of providing crèches or childcare that would allow families to access such services:

"Crèche facilities always seem lacking whenever one tries to kickstart a new project."

"Childcare provision from nursery nurses while mums can receive support/ treatment."

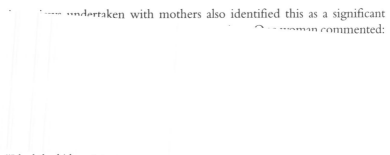

...... undertaken with mothers also identified this as a significant

.... woman commented:

"I had the kids and it meant training ...
the way back down."

Table 11.2: Valuable resources that are currently not available locally

	Number of times cited		
	Site A[a]	Site B[b]	Total
Support groups/mother and toddler groups/ women's centres	47	24	71
Crèche/childcare to allow mothers to access services	27	8	35
Drop-ins/community centres and clinics	20	15	35
Counselling/psychotherapy for mothers	24	7	31
Family support	16	14	30
Improved access to mental health services	21	7	28
Improved access to childcare	10	17	27
Family centre/assessment centre	10	16	26
Integrated/one-stop service	16	8	24
Local mother and baby unit	7	15	22
Crisis/24-hour emergency service	15	4	19
Respite care	7	11	18
Specialist team/worker	11	6	17
Services for older children	11	5	16
Residential unit/accommodation	9	6	15
Parenting groups	10	4	14
Counselling/therapy for children	7	–	7

Notes: [a] 191 respondents identified valuable resources in Site A.

[b] 108 respondents identified valuable resources in Site B.

Many of the suggestions reiterated the points made in response to the question concerning existing but inaccessible resources. Practitioners, particularly in research site A, argued that community mental health services needed to extend their eligibility criteria to include mothers with mental health needs and stressed that delays in service delivery were "unacceptable". Staff in both areas emphasised the need for more family support services, suggesting that family support staff needed to have access to skills and knowledge in mental health work:

> "Family support workers who have a good working knowledge of mental health problems."

> "Family centre with practitioner qualified in mental health as a support to mothers."

In fact, site A was, at the time of the survey, in the process of initiating a scheme for locating a community mental health worker in each family centre. However, it was clear that few practitioners were aware of this development at the point when they participated in the study. Some practitioners developed the theme of shared knowledge and services further with proposals for integrated systems in which mental health services could be delivered alongside family support in a 'one-stop' service:

> "A café specifically for mothers where alternative treatments and support could be provided, where child-minding, crèche or nursery facilities are also provided – a package of care and support."

An alternative model involved combining assessment and drop-in facilities:

> "Assessment centres which could provide mental health support – to meet CPNs, psychiatrists and social workers in the same unit. More informal drop-in facilities where children could attend, use for contact and where all professionals involved could observe mother and children together."

Such suggestions might serve as models for a family mental health service that aimed to meet a range of health and social needs for parents and children. Counselling or psychotherapy for mothers was also seen as a key component of an integrated package of family care:

> "A psychotherapy service for mothers which would be part of a coordinated package of treatment for the child and family."

The research interviews with mothers (see Chapter Seven of this book) also emphasised the value of counselling and psychotherapy services for those women who had received such help. In identifying a need for such services, practitioners recognised that counselling services needed to be culturally sensitive:

"Bilingual counselling service (particularly for female *and* male community).
Awareness of cultural issues impacting on health, as well as specific disorders
such as post-traumatic stress disorder."

This point was made by a number of respondents in relation to a range of services.

Overall, the professionals participating in the survey tended to identify
community-based services that were informal and flexible as being particularly
appropriate for families where mothers had mental health problems. Although
practitioners emphasised the need for appropriate residential settings, most of
͏ ͏ ͏ ͏ ͏ ͏ ͏ they described were supportive or preventive. There were concerns
͏ ͏ ͏ ͏ ͏ ͏ ͏ mothers to be

divides are helpful. As noted in Chapter ͏ ͏ ͏,
are heavily implicated in maternal mental health needs. Likewise, parental
needs and children's needs are intimately connected, if not always compatible.

The proposals for women-only mental health day services (DoH, 2000a)
might well meet some of the resource needs articulated by the survey respondents,
particularly those which involved providing flexible informal services with
childcare facilities attached. Women-only day services could also be targeted
appropriately in order to meet the needs of women whose mental health
problems were rooted in their experiences of abuse or in the stresses of parenting
on a low income and with little support. Currently, it appears that when
women's mental health problems are seen as explicable in terms of a history of
abuse or high levels of stress, support from mental health services may not be
accessed since the need is not defined as a mental health problem (Sheppard
with Kelly, 2001). However, women-only mental health day services would
not necessarily provide any response to the difficulties in interprofessional
communication and coordination detailed in Chapter Ten of this book. Such
problems are more likely to be resolved by services that are interprofessional in
their organisation or by structures specifically designed to promote coordination
and collaboration. We outline such a model in our concluding chapter.

TWELVE

Conclusion

This final chapter draws together the key themes of our research and develops some recommendations for policy and practice. The study findings have relevance for transactions between practitioners and users as well as for the

Therefore, the messages here are aimed at the full range of practitioners in statutory and voluntary settings.

The centrality of trust

The interviews with mothers highlighted their capacity to distinguish clearly between different professionals and their primary responsibilities. Mothers were aware that child care social workers' predominant task was the protection of children's welfare. They resented the scrutiny of their parenting by child care social workers and experienced child protection case conferences, supervised contact and other formal processes as threatening and disempowering. Such accounts are consonant with the evidence of other research studies (Cleaver and Freeman, 1995; Farmer and Owen, 1995) that have explored families' perspectives on the child protection process. However, for mothers with mental health problems, the alienation and powerlessness experienced in relation to the child protection system are likely to exacerbate existing feelings of low self-esteem, loss of control and stigma.

The women in this study also criticised child care social workers' lack of availability and the attitudes they displayed towards service users. Such comments may in part be a response to the statutory role of child care social workers with its implicit threat of coercion; however, they also reflect child care social workers' limited opportunities for the exercise of interpersonal and counselling skills in the job. These restrictions can be attributed to a combination of limited resources and an emphasis on a bureaucratic, care management model of practice that prioritises assessment and the construction of care packages over therapeutic interactions with service users. Child care social workers acknowledged the difficulties they had in providing the listening and counselling input that mothers clearly valued. It was also notable that practitioners did not seem to value the attitudes they communicated to their clients as highly or as consistently as mothers did. All practitioners were less likely to cite professionals' attitudes as important to mothers and were more likely to identify resources and support as central to responding to mothers' needs.

In their emphasis on being accorded respect and being listened to, the mothers interviewed were no different from countless other users of social work services who have told researchers what they wanted from services. The earliest and most celebrated of such accounts is Mayer and Timms' study, *The client speaks* (1970). The growth of organisations representing users' views and experiences over the past 20 years has produced a body of work detailing service users' experiences and critiques of services. Such accounts are relevant for both health and social care services. In addition to a focus on rights and participation, this body of literature stresses the importance of practitioners' attitudes and interpersonal skills. When asked to develop standards for social care practitioners, service users identified:

> people who are experienced and well informed, able to explain things clearly
> and without condescension and who 'really listen' .... (Harding and Beresford,
> 1996, p 1)

The women in our study saw community mental health workers as more able to provide the support and attitudes they valued. This was partly because they were perceived as being 'on their side', but also because they offered the attitudes, listening skills and accessibility that promoted the development of trust. As we noted earlier, the existence of a close confiding relationship can act as a protective buffer against the development of depression. While the research of Brown and his colleagues, discussed in Chapter One of this book, does not explore the capacity of professionals to provide such relationships, health and social care services may be a primary source of such support in communities where social support networks are limited by high levels of deprivation. There was some evidence from the interviews with mothers who had received counselling or therapeutic interventions from mental health professionals such as community psychiatric nurses (CPNs), mental health resource centre workers and psychologists, that this input had been significant in enabling them to reframe their difficulties and assert some control over their lives.

There was less evidence available from the interviews concerning the work of other professional groups. Psychiatrists tended to be perceived as remote male authority figures and were rarely mentioned in any positive light. General practitioners were seen as having only limited time and interest, probably an accurate reflection of the extent of their involvement in mothers' mental health, which is restricted by their wide remit and responsibilities. Other professionals featured only infrequently in the women's accounts of services. However, the expansion in family support services that has largely taken place since the completion of the study, and the development of multidisciplinary initiatives such as Sure Start, are likely to bring a wider range of professionals into contact with families where mothers have mental health needs.

In the absence of trust, women found that the child protection system mirrored the oppressive and threatening nature of mental health problems. They also indicated that negative experiences of child care services could deter them from seeking help for their mental health problems as they judged that sharing information about their mental health needs could jeopardise their continued care of their children. This suggests that problems may need to escalate to crisis point before services get involved, increasing the likelihood of coercive ⋯⋯ in the form of both compulsory admission to psychiatric care ⋯⋯ at an early stage also

after children, relationships with other and the question of substitute care in the event of future mental health crises need to be addressed in the context of a relationship of trust. It was evident that the absence of such partnerships with child care social work contributed to making such matters exceptionally stressful and demanding for mothers and children. For some of the women interviewed, anxieties and uncertainties about contact and placements represented additional sources of stress on an ongoing basis and could be conceptualised within the framework of Brown and Harris' (1978) theory of depression as a vulnerability factor that entailed ongoing difficulties and contributed to low self-esteem. The damaging consequences for mothers' mental health over time could be considerable.

Mothers' ambivalence about involvement with services, particularly statutory child care services, is likely to be communicated to the professionals involved. The limited availability of child care social workers may follow in part from the perception that they are not welcome and are experienced as intrusive in such families. A lack of confidence in responding to mental health problems may compound such feelings. However, high demands on child care social workers' time combined with staff shortages in many areas are likely to be equally relevant in limiting their availability and accessibility.

One significant development since our research was completed has been the implementation of the new *Framework for the assessment of children in need and their families* (DoH et al, 2000). The holistic approach underpinning the framework should encourage child care social workers to broaden their focus away from a negative preoccupation with parental mental health problems to take account of other factors and potential strengths in the family, while also recognising the impact of mental health problems on parenting. However, the framework could also be used as a bureaucratic tool to impede interpersonal interaction with families. Commentators have noted the static nature of the framework (Sidebotham, 2001) and of the social work approach to the assessment of parenting generally (Woodcock, 2003). An assessment that occurs at a fixed point in time may not be particularly appropriate for mothers with fluctuating mental health needs.

The *Framework for the assessment of children in need and their families* was designed as an interprofessional tool with the aim of drawing a range of practitioners into the task of assessment. Where parents have mental health needs, the circle of professionals involved will extend beyond child care and primary health staff to include community mental health workers and perhaps those professionals in secondary health settings. Therefore, the issue of interprofessional communication is fundamental, especially since risk assessment and management require coordination of information and service provision. The original objectives established for the study involved the identification of weaknesses in interprofessional networks and potential solutions to such problems, and we will move on to consider the findings relating to this area.

Interprofessional communication

The survey data identified the weakest lines of communication as those between GPs and child care social workers and between adult psychiatrists and child care social work. This finding echoes those of other research studies which have located a number of difficulties in interprofessional work in child protection with medical practitioners (Hallett, 1995; Lupton et al, 2001). These problems have been attributed to a range of factors, including unrealistic expectations from other practitioners, varying work practices and responsibilities and differentials in status and knowledge base. Problems with confidentiality were also identified as relevant by the survey and these followed the same interprofessional patterns as the difficulties of coordination described by respondents.

Difficulties in coordinating work with GPs may result in failures to access specialist mental health services for service users. Some commentators (Hallett and Birchall, 1992) have suggested that GPs have little to contribute to child protection processes and decisions. For mothers who have mental health needs, however, they represent the front line of mental health care in the community and the gateway to specialist services. Should GPs be unable to contribute to interprofessional decision making and planning and opt to be represented by other professionals in interagency forums, such arrangements need to be formally and explicitly acknowledged. Those acting on behalf of GPs require clarity about the information and resources they are able to contribute to assessment and planning processes.

The difficulties experienced in coordinating work with adult psychiatrists are also particularly relevant when mothers have mental health problems. Other professionals as well as mothers may share a sense that the psychiatrist is remote from the concerns of families. The practitioners participating in the focus groups described in Chapter Five of this book conveyed an ambivalence concerning psychiatric diagnosis, and described unease with the labels conferred by psychiatrists as well as a simultaneous desire for clear messages about an individual's needs and problems. Our pilot study (Stanley and Penhale, 1999) included examples of social workers asking adult psychiatrists to assess mothers' parenting capacity. The high status of medical practitioners may give rise to confusion about the appropriate contribution of psychiatric expertise to the assessment of parenting. Child care social workers need to be clear about the extent of psychiatric expertise and to recognise that adult psychiatrists are able to assess a mother's mental health problems but will not necessarily have any

significant part in assess parenting capacity. Reder and

coordinating role. While it was apparent that professionals were able to acknowledge other groups' rights to take a lead in this area – and there was some degree of consensus concerning child care social workers' key role in such work – the survey did not identify one professional group as the outright favourite for this task.

Families require both sensitive psychological support for parents and monitoring of children's welfare where mothers' mental health problems and child protection concerns coexist. The research findings indicate that the former task is best undertaken by community mental health workers, such as CPNs, mental health social workers and mental health resource centre staff, while the latter remains the domain of child care staff. Mental health services are not without their coercive elements, and child care social work is moving increasingly towards supporting the needs of families, but the primary client focus of the two services clearly differs. Child care social workers appear to lack the capacity to offer mothers the emotional support they define as effective. Our study identified a concurrence between practitioners' and service users' views on this issue. On the other hand, it is clear that children living in families where mothers have mental health problems may need additional support and, in some cases, may be at risk of significant harm. These dual sets of interconnected needs argue the case for a dyad of community mental health and child care workers to work together to coordinate assessment and services for these families.

Such a dyad would offer adults' and children's services a shared keyworker role. This type of joint arrangement would facilitate insight into the procedures, legal provisions and interventions specific to different services. Community mental health workers might also assume a particular role in facilitating communication between child care workers and adult psychiatry (Tye and

Precey, 1999). This could involve clarification of the function and limits of diagnosis as well as promoting dialogue. While questions concerning confidentiality and client focus would on an ongoing basis need to be addressed, a close working relationship between two nominated professionals might serve to ensure that such issues were explicitly addressed rather than remaining unacknowledged and problematic.

This approach also has the potential to promote increased clarity and specificity for families in relation to the contrasting roles assumed by the two keyworkers. The different professional responsibilities could translate into one practitioner acting as supportive confidante, while the other emphasised monitoring and the protection of children. The success of this model will rest on the degree of openness and coordination achieved between the two keyworkers. Our survey of practitioners indicated that there were grounds for optimism concerning professionals' capacity to engage with the needs and viewpoints of family members other than their primary client group. Additionally, community mental health workers and child care social workers appeared positive about their capacity to coordinate work with one another.

Allocating a dyad of workers to a family would represent a significant demand on resources for services, but would also avoid the problems that arise when one agency withdraws support on the grounds that another service is involved. Should open communication be extended beyond the partnership between keyworkers to include family members, much might be achieved towards ensuring partnerships with families and relationships characterised by trust.

Imminent changes in the structures of mental health and child care services become relevant when advocating such a model. Our approach emphasises collaboration between community-based mental health services and child care professionals. It can be contrasted with other models, such as Reder et al's (2000c) suggestion of a partnership between child and adult psychiatrists which would entail closer working between those in clinical settings. As both mental health and child care services move towards integration into separate trusts, the gap between them is likely to widen, making proposals for a family psychiatry service appear even less likely to be translated into reality. The model proposed here acknowledges the existence of the divide between children's and adults' services and offers a means of bridging it.

Flexible services

A shortfall in preventive services in either mental health or child care can result in professionals needing to over-emphasise risks in order to access those services that are available. When a locality lacks accessible resources that can be informally accessed without recourse to statutory services, mothers' tendencies to avoid using services until a crisis point is reached will be reinforced. This can be described as a damaging form of collusion between rationed services and service users that precludes early interventions.

The study indicated some of the ways in which services could be made more relevant and accessible to families where mothers have mental health needs. A need for childcare facilities while women received appropriate therapeutic or psychological support was apparent, but wider access to childcare generally was also advocated. Indeed, as seen in Chapter Nine of this book, professionals saw resources to assist parenting as the most important need that mothers might have. Flexible forms of childcare emerged as key in meeting both specialist mental health or psychological needs and broader needs relating to social exclusion.

The other significant theme in the data concerning resources was the emphasis on opportunities for children and parents to access services in the same setting.

models advocated by surrey councils of one-stop services for parents with mental health needs and their children and included suggestions for respite or residential care for the whole family.

While the re-focusing of child care social work has aimed to ensure that risk is no longer the key to unlocking services for families, such a shift cannot be achieved in practice without additional resources. Additional resources have been made available through 'Quality Protects' monies and central government funding for area-based initiatives such as Sure Start. Mental health services are currently targeted on high-risk groups but the consultative document on a national strategy for women's mental health (DoH, 2002a) acknowledges that women's mental health problems are more likely to be classified as neurotic and as located in their social circumstances. Services need to be more freely available to those whose needs are so defined without a label of risk or danger needing to be attached. The national strategy also signals a shift towards a more family-friendly mental health service. Such a service might incorporate crèche facilities in mental health settings, the provision of crisis accommodation for families, domiciliary and childcare support delivered in the home, counselling or psychotherapy services and support and self-help groups for mothers with mental health problems.

Interprofessional training

The survey of professionals provided evidence for the enduring nature of difficulties in interprofessional communication and the resilience of professional tribalism and self-interest. Training programmes have been advocated as a means of improving interprofessional collaboration, breaking down stereotypes and developing understanding of other professionals' perspectives and roles, as well as building skills in detecting mental health needs and childcare concerns (Falkov, 1998; McClure and Wells, 2000). Our experience of delivering such courses suggests that joint training programmes that include a wide range of practitioners from health, social services and the voluntary sector can be effective in this respect. However, such courses will only work for those who attend them and there is a long history of failure in securing the attendance of medical staff at such training events.

Much interprofessional training in this area has been coordinated by local ACPCs, which, as their critics are increasingly noting, lack any formal powers to require agencies to work together or even attend interprofessional training. The limited funding available to ACPCs also makes it difficult for them to offer self-employed professionals, such as GPs, financial incentives to participate in such events. At the time of writing, it looks likely that ACPCs will either have their powers reinforced or will be replaced by new and more powerful bodies. However, given the many demands on medical practitioners at present, particularly those in primary care, interprofessional training is likely to continue to be a low priority for them.

Maintaining a dual focus

Many of the problems in delivering effective services to families where mothers have mental health needs appear to arise from difficulties in maintaining a dual focus on women. They are both adults, with their own set of needs, and parents, responsible for meeting the needs of dependent children and guaranteeing their safety. The available evidence, laden with connotations of risk and dangerousness, has been interpreted as emphasising adverse effects for children whose mothers have mental health problems. The message communicated to practitioners is that one set of needs will almost always need to be sacrificed if the other is to be met.

A dual focus might involve identifying a woman's abusive past and the ways in which it affects her current functioning and her capacity to parent. Appropriate therapeutic services or other opportunities for developing self-esteem might be offered alongside careful monitoring of the children's welfare. However, most practitioners will find this dual approach demanding, particularly if local services are scarce. Tensions and difficulties in interprofessional work will increase the likelihood that services are unavailable. If mothers' needs are unmet, they are more likely to be perceived as threatening the safety of dependent children.

While recognition of a mother's dual identity (as a person and a parent) might be achieved by practitioners when risk is perceived as low, the ability to retain this dual focus over time is compromised once risk is assessed as high. This would appear likely to hold equally true whether the child or the mother is at risk. Should the woman's mental health be at crisis level, it may be almost impossible for mental health practitioners to maintain an appropriate level of vigilance in relation to children. Likewise, child care social workers may feel that children's safety is too precarious to wait for therapeutic support for mothers to be accessed and utilised. In each case, professionals' awareness of the potential for blame accruing to them as individuals may result in a narrow perspective focused on the needs of their primary client.

This difficulty in maintaining a dual focus constitutes an additional argument for the dyad of community mental health and child care workers proposed here. Each keyworker could assume primary responsibility for monitoring and working with one aspect of the mother's identity and needs. Fulfilling the demands of the parenting role while meeting one's own needs is a struggle for many women. The accommodation of the two sets of needs is often precarious and may rest on the availability of support from the extended family, local

these mothers are likely to remain involved in the care of their children and to play an important role in their lives. They will need help in parenting at a distance. Other women will continue to care for their children at home. For them, this approach might yield some creative solutions that encompass both practical and emotional forms of support. Perhaps, most importantly, such an approach would inform professional attitudes to mothers, attitudes that are respectful and non-judgmental. This, we have learned, is what women want.

References

Alaszewski, A. (2002) 'Risk and dangerousness', in B. Bytheway, V. Bacigalupo, J. Bornat, J. Johnson and S. Spurr (eds) *Understanding care, welfare and community: A reader*, London: Routledge, pp 183-91.

Aldridge, J. and Becker, S. (2003) *Children caring for parents with mental illness: Perspectives of young carers, parents and professionals*, Bristol: The Policy Press.

', *British Journal of*

participation by general practitioners in the child protection preliminary conclusions from focus group discussions in West Midlands, UK', *Journal of Interprofessional Care*, vol 13, no 3, pp 239-48.

Barbour, R.S. (1999) 'Are focus groups an appropriate tool for studying organizational change?', in R.S. Barbour and J. Kitzinger (eds) *Developing focus group research: Politics, theory and practice*, London: Sage Publications, pp 113-26.

Barbour, R.S., Stanley, N., Penhale, B. and Holden, S. (2002) 'Assessing risk: professional perspectives on work involving mental health and child care services', *Journal of Interprofessional Care*, vol 16, no 4, pp 323-34.

Barclay, P. (1982) *Social workers: Their role and tasks*, London: Bedford Square Press.

Barham, P. (1992) *Closing the asylum: The mental patient in modern society*, London: Penguin.

Baylis, G. (2002) *Mental health grant guidelines prove difficult to implement*, London: YoungMinds.

Beck, U. (1992) *The risk society: Towards a new modernity*, London: Sage Publications.

Becker, H.S. (1977) *Sociological work: Method and substance*, New Jersey: Transaction.

Becker, S. (2000) 'Young carers in the UK: research, policy and practice', *Research Policy and Planning*, vol 18, no 2, pp 13-22.

Becker, S., Aldridge, J. and Dearden, C. (1998) *Young carers and their families*, Oxford: Blackwell Science.

Beresford, P. and Wallcraft, J. (1997) 'Psychiatric system survivors and emancipatory research: issues, overlaps and differences', in C. Barnes and G. Mercer (eds) *Doing disability research*, Leeds: The Disability Press, pp 67-87.

Bernard, J. and Douglas, A. (1999) 'The size of the task facing professional agencies', in A. Weir and A. Douglas (eds) *Child protection and adult mental health: Conflict of interest*, Oxford: Butterworth Heinemann, pp 109-36.

Bifulco, A. and Moran, P. (1998) *Wednesday's child: Research into women's experiences of neglect and abuse in childhood, and adult depression*, London: Routledge.

Birchall, E. with Hallett, C. (1995) *Working together in child protection*, London: HMSO.

Blom-Cooper, L., Grounds, A., Guinan, P., Parker, A. and Taylor, M. (1996) *The case of Jason Mitchell: Report of the independent panel of inquiry*, London: Duckworth.

Bloor, M., Frankland, J., Thomas, M. and Robson, K. (2001) *Focus groups in social research*, London: Sage Publications.

Bollas, C. (2001) 'The misapplication of "reasonable mindedness": is psychoanalysis possible with present reporting laws in the USA and UK?', in C. Cordess (ed) *Confidentiality and mental health*, London: Jessica Kingsley, pp 109-18.

Bowers, L. (2002) *Dangerous and severe personality disorder: Response and role of the psychiatric team*, London: Routledge.

Boyd, W. (1996) *Report of the confidential inquiry into homicides and suicides by mentally ill people*, London: Royal College of Psychiatrists.

Broverman, K., Broverman, D., Clarkson, F., Rosenkrantz, P. and Vogel, S. (1970) 'Sex-role stereotyping and clinical judgement of mental health', *Journal of Consulting and Clinical Psychology*, vol 34, pp 1-7.

Brown, G.W. (1996) 'Life events, loss and depressive disorders', in T. Heller, J. Reynolds, R. Gomm, R. Muston and S. Pattison (eds) *Mental health matters: A reader*, Basingstoke: Macmillan with the Open University, pp 36-45.

Brown, G.W. and Harris, T.O. (1978) *The social origins of depression: A study of psychiatric disorder in women*, London: Tavistock Publications.

Brown, G.W., Bifulco, A. and Andrews, B. (1990) 'Self esteem and depression: 3. Aetiological issues', *Social Psychiatry and Psychiatric Epidemiology*, vol 25, pp 235-43.

Brown, G.W., Andrews, B., Harris, T., Adler, Z. and Bridget, L. (1986) 'Social support, self-esteem and depression', *Psychological Medicine*, vol 16, pp 813-31.

Brown, G.W., Harris, T.O., Hepworth, C. and Robinson, R. (1994) 'Clinical and psychosocial origins of chronic depression. 2. A patient enquiry', *British Journal of Psychiatry*, vol 165, pp 457-65.

Bullock, R., Little, M. and Milham, S. (1993) *Going home: The return of children separated from their families*, Aldershot: Dartmouth.

Busfield, J. (1996) *Men, women and madness: Understanding gender and mental disorder*, London: Macmillan.

Butler-Sloss, E. (1988) *Report on the inquiry into child abuse in Cleveland 1987*, Cm 412, London: HMSO

Cawson, P., Wattam, C., ... the United Kingdom, London: NSPCC.

Chesler, P. (1972) *Women and madness*, New York: Doubleday.

Chief Inspector of Social Services, Director for Health Improvement, Commission for Health Improvement, Her Majesty's Chief Inspectors of the Crown Prosecution Service, Her Majesty's Chief Inspector of the Magistrates' Courts Service, Her Majesty's Chief Inspector of Schools, Her Majesty's Chief Inspector of Prisons and Her Majesty's Chief Inspector of Probation (2002) *Safeguarding children: A joint Chief Inspectors' report on arrangements to safeguard children*, London: DoH.

Cleaver, H. and Freeman, P. (1995) *Parental perspectives in cases of suspected child abuse*, London: HMSO.

Cleaver, H., Unnell, I. and Aldgate, J. (1999) *Children's needs – Parenting capacity: The impact of parental mental illness, problem alcohol and drug use and domestic violence on children's development*, London: The Stationery Office.

Colton, M., Drury, C. and Williams, M. (1995) *Children in need: Family support under the Children Act 1989*, Aldershot: Avebury.

Confidential Inquiries into Maternal Deaths in the United Kingdom (2001) *Why mothers die 1997-1999*, London: National Institute for Clinical Excellence.

Corby, B. (2000) *Child abuse: Towards a knowledge base* (2nd edn), Buckingham: Open University Press.

Corby, B. (2002) 'Inter-professional cooperation and inter-agency coordination', in K. Wilson and A. James (eds) *The child protection handbook* (2nd edn), London: Ballière Tindall, pp 272-87.

Corby, B., Millar, M. and Pope, A. (2002) 'Assessing children in need assessments – a parental perspective', *Practice*, vol 14, no 4, pp 5-16.

Corney, R. (1990) 'A survey of professional help sought by patients for psychosocial problems', *British Journal of General Practice*, vol 40, pp 365-8.

Corney, R. and Strathdee, G. (1996) 'Developing primary care services for women', in K. Abel, M. Buszewicz, S. Davison, S. Johnson and E. Staples (eds) *Planning community mental health services for women: A multiprofessional handbook*, London: Routledge, pp 191-201.

Coward, R. (1997) 'The heaven and the hell of mothering: mothering and ambivalence in the mass media', in W. Hollway and B. Featherstone (eds) *Mothering and ambivalence*, London: Routledge, pp 111-18.

Cox, A.D. (1993) 'Befriending young mothers', *British Journal of Psychiatry*, vol 163, pp 6-18.

Cox, A.D., Puckering, C., Pound, A. and Mills, M. (1987) 'The impact of maternal depression in young children', *Child Psychology and Psychiatry*, vol 22, no 6, pp 917-28.

Cox, A.D., Puckering, C., Pound, A. and Mills, M. (1991) 'Evaluation of a lone visiting befriending service for young mothers: NEWPIN', *Journal of the Royal College of Medicine*, vol 84, pp 217-20.

Cox, J. and Holden, J. (eds) (1994) *Perinatal psychiatry: Use and misuse of the Edinburgh postnatal scale*, London: Gaskell.

Crawford, L., Devaux, M., Ferris, R. and Hayward, P. (1997) *The report into the care and treatment of Martin Mursell*, London: Camden and Islington Health Authority.

Crow, G. and Hardey, M. (1991) 'The housing strategies of lone parents', in M. Hardey and G. Crow (eds) *Lone parenthood: Coping with constraints and making opportunities*, Hemel Hempstead: Harvester Wheatsheaf.

Dalley, G. (1989) 'Professional ideology or organisational tribalism? The health service–social work divide', in R. Taylor and J. Ford (eds) *Social work and health care*, London: Jessica Kingsley, pp 102-17.

Daniel, B. and Taylor, J. (2001) *Engaging with fathers: Practice issues for health and social care*, London: Jessica Kingsley.

Davies, M. and Woolgrove, M. (1998) 'Mental health social work and the use of supervision registers for patients at risk', *Health and Social Care in the Community*, vol 6, no 1, pp 25-34.

Deakin, N. (2001) 'Public policy, social policy and voluntary organisations', in M. Harris and C. Rochester (eds) *Voluntary organisations and social policy in Britain: Perspectives on change and choice*, Basingstoke: Palgrave, pp 21-36.

Dearden, C. and Becker, S. (2000) *Growing up caring: Vulnerability and transition to adulthood – young carers' experiences*, York: Joseph Rowntree Foundation.

DHSS (Department of Health and Social Security) (1974) *Report of the committee of inquiry into the care and supervision provided in relation to Maria Colwell*, London: HMSO.

~~~~ ~~~~ ~~~~ *~~~~ of child care law: Report to ministers of an interdepartmental*

DoH (1991) *Child abuse: A study of inquiry reports ~~~~ ~~~~, ~~~~*

DoH (1994) *Introduction of supervision registers for mentally ill people* (HSG(94)5), London: DoH.

DoH (1995a) *Child protection: Messages from research*, London: HMSO.

DoH (1995b) *Building bridges: A guide to arrangements for inter-agency working for the care and protection of severely mentally ill people*, London: DoH.

DoH (1998a) *Modernising social services: Promoting independence, improving protection, raising standards*, Cm 4169, London: The Stationery Office.

DoH (1998b) *Quality protects: Framework for action*, London: DoH Social Care Group.

DoH (1999a) *Effective care co-ordination in mental health services: Modernising the care programme approach*, London: DoH.

DoH (1999b) *National Service Framework for Mental Health*, London: DoH.

DoH (1999c) *NHS modernisation fund and mental health grant for child and adolescent mental health services (CAMHS) 1999/2002* (HSC 2002/002: LAC(2002)3), London: DoH.

DoH (2000a) *The NHS Plan: A plan for investment, a plan for reform*, Cm 4818-1, London: The Stationery Office.

DoH (2000b) *Social services performance in 1999-2000*, London: Government Statistical Service and DoH.

DoH (2001) *Social services performance assessment framework indicators, 2000-2001*, London: Government Statistical Service and DoH.

DoH (2002a) *Women's mental health: Into the mainstream – Strategic development of mental health care for women*, London: DoH.

DoH (2002b) *Mental Health Bill: Consultation document*, Cm 5538-11, London: The Stationery Office.

DoH (2003) *Getting the right start: National service framework for children – Emerging findings*, London: DoH.

DoH, HO and DfEE (Department of Health, Home Office and Department for Education and Employment) (1999) *Working together to safeguard children*, London: The Stationery Office.

DoH, DfEE and HO (2000) *Framework for the assessment of children in need and their families*, London: The Stationery Office.

DoH and Welsh Office (1999) *Code of practice: Mental Health Act 1983*, London: The Stationery Office.

Dohrenwend, B. and Dohrenwend, B.S. (1977) 'Sex differences in mental illness: a reply to Gove and Tudor', *American Journal of Sociology*, vol 82, pp 1336-41.

Dolan, B. and Coid, J. (1993) *Psychopathic antisocial personality disorder*, London: Gaskell.

Double, V. (1998) *A difficult engagement: A report of the independent inquiry into the care and treatment of Alfina Magdalena Gabriel*, Huddersfield: Calderdale and Kirklees Health Authority.

Dumka, L.E., Gonzales, N.A., Wood, J.L. and Formoso, D. (1998) 'Using qualitative methods to develop contextually relevant measures and preventive interventions: an illustration', *American Journal of Community Psychology*, vol 26, no 4, pp 605-37.

DWP (Department for Work and Pensions) (2002) *Opportunity for all*, Cm 5598, London: The Stationery Office.

Ettore, E. (1992) *Women and substance use*, Basingstoke: Macmillan.

Falkov, A. (1996) *Study of working together 'Part 8' reports. Fatal child abuse and parental psychiatric disorder: An analysis of 100 area child protection committee case reviews conducted under the terms of Part 8 of Working together under the Children Act 1989*, London: DoH.

Falkov, A. (ed) (1998) *Crossing bridges: Training resources for working with mentally ill parents and their children*, Brighton: Pavilion Publishing.

Falkov, A. and Davies, N. (1997) 'Solutions on the ground: a family mental health service', in Michael Sieff Foundation, *Keeping children in mind: Balancing children's needs with parents' mental health. Report of 12th Annual Conference*, London: Michael Sieff Foundation.

Fallon, P., Bluglass, R., Edwards, B. and Daniels, G. (1999) *Report of the committee of inquiry into the personality disorder unit, Ashworth Special Hospital*, London: DoH.

Farmer, E. and Owen, M. (1995) *Child protection practice: Private risks and public remedies*, London: HMSO.

Finch, J. (1984) 'It's great to have someone to talk to: the ethics and politics of interviewing women', in C. Bell and H. Roberts (eds) *Social researching: Politics, problems and practice*, London: Routledge, pp 70-87.

Finkelhor, D. (1994) 'The international epidemiology of child sexual abuse', *Child Abuse and Neglect*, vol 18, no 5, pp 409-17.

Fox, S. and Dingwall, R. (1985) 'An exploratory study of variations in social workers' and health visitors' definitions of child mistreatment', *British Journal of Social Work*, vol 15, no 5, pp 467-78.

Fox Harding, L. (1997) *Perspectives in child care policy* (2nd edn), London: Longman.

Fulford, B. (2001) 'The paradoxes of confidentiality: a philosophical introduction', in C. Cordess (ed) *Confidentiality and mental health*, London: Jessica Kingsley, pp 7-23.

Ghate, D., Shaw, C. and Hazel, N. (2000) *Fathers and family centres: Engaging fathers in preventive services*, London: Policy Research Bureau.

Gibbons, J., Conroy, S. and Bell, C. (1995) *Operating the child protection system*, London: HMSO.

Giovannoni, J. and Becerra, R. (1979) *Defining child abuse*, New York: Free Press.

Glaser, D. and Prior, V. (1997) 'Is the term child protection applicable to emotional abuse?', *Child Abuse Review*, vol 6, pp 315-30.

Gold, J. (1998) 'Gender differences in psychiatric illness and treatments: a critical review', *Journal of Nervous and Mental Diseases*, vol 186, no 12, pp 769-75.

Goldberg, D.P. and Huxley, P. (1992) *Common mental disorders – A biopsychosocial model*, London: Routledge and Kegan Paul.

Golding, J. (1999) 'Intimate partner violence as a risk factor for mental disorders: a meta analysis', *Journal of Family Violence*, vol 14, pp 99-132.

Göpfert, M., Webster, J. and Seeman, M.V. (eds) (1996) *Parental psychiatric disorder*, Cambridge: Cambridge University Press.

Göpfert, M., Webster, J., Pollard, J. and Nelki, J. S. (1996) 'The assessment and prediction of parenting capacity: a community-oriented approach', in M. Göpfert, J. Webster and M.V. Seeman (eds) *Parental psychiatric disorder*, Cambridge: Cambridge University Press, pp 271-309.

Green, R. and Hyde, E. (1997) 'Integrating service users' views', Paper presented at 'Caught in the Acts' Conference, London: Pavilion Publishing.

Grounds, A. (1995) 'Risk assessment and management in clinical context', in J. Crichton (ed) *Psychiatric patient violence: Risk and response*, London: Duckworth, pp 43-59.

Hallett, C. (1995) *Interagency coordination in child protection*, London: HMSO.

Hallett, C. and Birchall, E. (1992) *Coordination and child protection: A review of the literature*, Edinburgh: HMSO.

Hallett, C. and Stevenson, O. (1980) *Child abuse: Aspects of inter-professional co-operation*, London: Allen & Unwin.

Harbour, A. (2001) 'The limits of confidentiality: a legal view', in C. Cordess (ed) *Confidentiality and mental health*, London: Jessica Kingsley.

Harbour, A., Brunning, J., Bolter, L. and Hally, H. (1996) *The Viner report*, Ferndown: Dorset Health Commission.

Harding, T. and Beresford, P. (1996) *The standards we expect: What service users and carers want from social services workers*, London: National Institute for Social Work.

Harris, M. and Rochester, C. (eds) (2001) *Voluntary organisations and social policy in Britain: Perspectives on change and choice*, Basingstoke: Palgrave.

Health Advisory Service (1995) *Together we stand: The commissioning role and management of child and adolescent mental health services*, London: HMSO.

Henricson, C., Katz, I., Mesie, J., Sandison, M. and Tunstill, J. (2001) *National mapping of family services in England and Wales – Consultation document*, London: National Family and Parenting Institute.

Hetherington, R., Baistow, K., Johansen, P. and Mesie, J. (1999) *The Icarus project: Professional intervention for mentally ill parents and their children. Building a European model*, Uxbridge: Brunel University.

Hetherington, R., Baistow, K., Katz, I. Mesie, J. and Trowell, J. (2001) *The welfare of children with mentally ill parents: Learning from inter-country comparisons*, Chichester: Wiley.

Hills, J. (1998) *Income and wealth: The latest evidence*, York: Joseph Rowntree Foundation.

Hugman, R. and Phillips, N. (1993) '"Like bees round the honeypot": social work responses to parents with mental health needs', *Practice*, vol 6, no 3, pp 193-205.

Humphreys, C. and Thiara, R. (2003) 'Mental health and domestic violence: "I call it symptoms of abuse"', *British Journal of Social Work*, vol 33, no 2, pp 209-26.

Ismail, K. (1996) 'Planning services for black women', in K. Abel, M. Buszewicz, S. Davison, S. Johnson and E. Staples (eds) *Planning community mental health services for women: A multiprofessional handbook*, London: Routledge, pp 65-78.

James, G. (1994) *Department of Health discussion report for ACPC conference: Study of Working Together Part 8 reports*, London: DoH.

Jenkins, J.H. (1996) 'The impress of extremity: women's experience of trauma and political violence', in C.F. Sargent and C.B. Brettell (eds) *Gender and health: An international perspective*, Upper Saddle River, NJ: Prentice Hall.

Jenkins, R., McCulloch, A., Friedl, L. and Parker, C. (2002) *Developing a national mental health policy*, Hove: Psychology Press.

Jeyarajah Dent, R. and McIntyre, C. (2000) 'Health visitors, children and parental mental health problems', in P. Reder, M. McClure and A. Jolley (eds) *Family matters: Interfaces between child and adult mental health*, London: Routledge, pp 180-91.

Johnson, S. and Buszewicz, M. (1996) 'Women's mental health in the UK', in K. Abel, M. Buszewicz, S. Davison, S. Johnson and E. Staples (eds) *Planning community mental health services for women,* London: Routledge, pp 6-19.

Jumper, S. (1995) 'A meta-analysis of the relationship of child sexual abuse to adult psychological adjustment', *Child Abuse and Neglect,* vol 19, no 6, pp 715-28.

Keating, F. (2002) 'Black-led initiatives in mental health: an overview', *Research Policy and Planning,* vol 20, no 2, pp 9-19.

Kemshall, H. (2002) *Risk, social policy and welfare,* Buckingham: Open University Press.

Kendall, L. and Harker, L. (eds) (with Davies, A., Harker, L., Hughes, L. Kendall, L., McTernan, J. and Wistow, G.) (2002) *From welfare to wellbeing: The future of social care,* London: Institute for Public Policy Research.

Kiernan, K., Land, H. and Lewis, J. (1997) *Lone motherhood in twentieth century Britain,* Oxford: Oxford University Press.

Kitzinger, J. (1995) 'Introducing focus groups', *British Medical Journal,* vol 311, pp 299-302.

Kitzinger, J. and Barbour, R.S. (1999) 'Introduction: the challenge and promise of focus groups', in R.S. Barbour and J. Kitzinger (eds) *Developing focus group research: Politics, theory and practice,* London: Sage Publications, pp 1-20.

Kohen, D. (2000) 'Introduction', in D. Kohen (ed) *Women and mental health,* London: Brunner-Routledge, pp 1-16.

Laming, H. (2003) *The Victoria Climbié inquiry,* Cm 5730, London: The Stationery Office.

Lindsay, M., Potter, R. and Shepperd, A. (1999) 'Managing strategies for change in child care and mental health services in Bath and north east Somerset', in A. Weir and A. Douglas (eds) *Child protection and adult mental health: Conflict of interest?,* Oxford: Butterworth and Heinemann, pp 173-81.

London Borough of Brent (1985) *A child in trust: Report of the panel of inquiry investigating the circumstances surrounding the death of Jasmine Beckford,* London: London Borough of Brent.

London Borough of Greenwich (1987) *A child in mind: Protection of children in a responsible society. Report of the commission of inquiry into the circumstances surrounding the death of Kimberley Carlile,* London: London Borough of Greenwich.

London Borough of Lambeth (1987) *Whose child? The report of the panel appointed to inquire into the death of Tyra Henry,* London: London Borough of Lambeth.

Lupton, C., Khan, P., North, N. and Lacey, D. (1999) *The role of health professionals in the child protection process*, Report No 41, Portsmouth: Social Sciences Research and Information Unit, University of Portsmouth.

Lupton, C., North, N. and Khan, P. (2001) *Working together or pulling apart? The National Health Service and child protection networks*, Bristol: The Policy Press.

Lymbery, M. and Millward, A. (2000) 'The primary health care interface', in G. Bradley and J. Manthorpe (eds) *Working on the fault line*, Birmingham: Venture Press, pp 11-44.

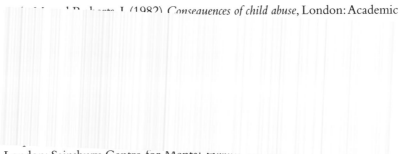

... and Roberts, J. (1982) *Consequences of child abuse*, London: Academic

London: Sainsbury Centre for Mental Health, pp 3-9.

McCulloch, A. and Parker, C. (2004: forthcoming) 'Mental health inquiries, assertive outreach and compliance', in N. Stanley and J. Manthorpe (eds) *The age of inquiries: Learning and blaming in health and social care*, London: Routledge.

Maitra, B. and Jolley, A. (2000) 'Liaison between child and adult psychiatric services', in P. Reder, M. McClure and A. Jolley (eds) *Family matters: Interfaces between child and adult mental health*, London: Routledge, pp 285-300.

Manthorpe, J. and Iliffe, S. (2003) 'Professional predictions: June Huntington's perspectives on joint working, 20 years on', *Journal of Interprofessional Care*, vol 17, no 1, pp 85-94.

Marsh, A., Ford, R. and Finlayson, L. (1997) *Lone parents*, London: The Stationery Office.

Mayer, J.E. and Timms, N. (1970) *The client speaks: Working class impressions of casework*, London: Routledge and Kegan Paul.

Meltzer, H. and Gatward, R. with Goodman, R. and Ford, T. (1999) *Mental health of children and adolescents in Great Britain*, London: The Stationery Office.

Meltzer, H., Gill, B., Petticrew, M. and Hinds, K. (1995) *The prevalence of psychiatric morbidity among adults living in private households*, London: HMSO.

Mental Health Foundation (1999) *Bright futures: Promoting children and young people's mental health*, London: Mental Health Foundation.

Michael Sieff Foundation (1997) *Keeping children in mind: Balancing children's needs with parents' mental health. Report of 12th Annual Conference*, London: Michael Sieff Foundation.

Milner, J. (1993) 'A disappearing act: the different career paths of fathers and mothers in child protection investigations', *Critical Social Policy*, vol 38, no 13.2, pp 48-63.

Mishcon, J., Mason, L. Stanner, S., Dick, D. and Mackay, J. (1997) *Report of the Independent Inquiry into the Treatment and Care of Doris Walsh*, Coventry: Coventry Health Authority.

Morrison, T. (2000) 'Working together to safeguard children: challenges and changes for inter-agency co-ordination in child protection', *Journal of Interprofessional Care*, vol 4, no 4, pp 363-74.

Mullen, P.E., Martin, J.L., Anderson, J.C., Romans, S.E. and Herbison, G.P. (1993) 'Childhood sexual abuse and mental health in adult life', *British Journal of Psychiatry*, vol 163, pp 721-32.

Mullins, D. and Riseborough, M. (2001) 'Non-profit housing agencies: reading and shaping the policy agenda', in M. Harris and C. Rochester (eds) *Voluntary organisations and social policy in Britain: Perspectives on change and choice*, Basingstoke: Palgrave, pp 154-70.

Munro, E. (2002) *Effective child protection*, London: Sage Publications.

Munro, E. (2004: forthcoming) 'The impact of child abuse inquiries since 1990', in N. Stanley and J. Manthorpe (eds) *The age of inquiries: Learning and blaming in health and social care*, London: Routledge.

Murray, L., Hipwell, A. and Hooper, R. (1996) 'Cognitive development of 5-year-old children of postnatally depressed mothers', *Child Psychology and Psychiatry*, vol 37, no 8, pp 927-35.

Murrell, L. (1999) 'Competing needs: working relationships between children and families and mental health social workers', *Kent Journal of Practice Research*, vol 4, Canterbury: Kent Social Services Strategy Group.

Neumann, D., Houskamp, B., Pollock, V. and Briere, J. (1996) 'The long-term sequelae of childhood sexual abuse in women: a meta-analytic review', *Child Maltreatment*, vol 1, no 1, pp 6-16.

Nicholson, J., Sweeney, E.M., Geller, J.L. (1998) 'Mothers with mental illness: I. The competing demands of parenting and living with mental illness', *Psychiatric Services*, vol 49, no 5, pp 635-42.

O'Hagan, K. and Dillenburger, K. (1995) *The abuse of women within childcare work*, Buckingham: Open University Press.

Olsen, R. and Wates, M. (2003) *Disabled parents: Examining research assumptions*, Dartington: Research in Practice.

ONS (Office for National Statistics) (2000) *Psychiatric morbidity among adults living in private households*, London: The Stationery Office.

Øvretveit, J. (1997) 'Evaluating interprofessional working – a case example of a community mental health team', in J. Øvretveit, P. Mathias and T. Thompson (eds) *Interprofessional working for health and social care*, Basingstoke: Macmillan, pp 57-78.

.... D. .. d Oppenheimer, R. (1992) 'Childhood sexual

London: Macmillan.

Parton, N. (2002) 'Protecting children: a socio-historical analysis', in K. Wilson and A. James (eds) *The child protection handbook* (2nd edn), London: Ballière Tindall, pp 11-28.

Pearce, J. (2003) 'Training update: parental mental health and child protection – making the links through training', *Child Abuse Review*, vol 12, no 2, pp 114-18.

Peck, E., Towell, D. and Gulliver, P. (2001) 'The meanings of "culture" in health and social care: a case study of the combined Trust in Somerset', *Interprofessional Care*, vol 15, no 4, pp 319-28.

Pilgrim, D. and Rogers, A. (1999) *A sociology of mental health and illness* (2nd edn), Buckingham: Open University Press.

Poulton, B.C. and West, M.A. (1999) 'The determinants of effectiveness in primary care teams', *Journal of Interprofessional Care*, vol 13, no 1, pp 7-18.

Powell, R.B., Hollander, D. and Tobansky, R.I. (1995) 'Crisis in admission beds: a four-year survey of the bed state of greater London's acute psychiatric units', *British Journal of Psychiatry*, vol 167, pp 765-9.

Prior, P. (1999) *Gender and mental health*, Basingstoke: Macmillan.

Quinton, D. and Rutter, M. (1985) 'Family pathology and child psychiatric disorder: a four-year prospective study', in A.R. Nicol (ed) *Longitudinal studies in child psychology and psychiatry*, Chichester: John Wiley, pp 91-134.

Reder, P. and Duncan, S. (1999) *Lost innocents*, London: Routledge.

Reder, P., McClure, M. and Jolley, A. (eds) (2000a) *Family matters: Interfaces between child and adult mental health*, London: Routledge.

Reder, P., McClure, M. and Jolley, A. (2000b) 'Interfaces between child and adult mental health', in P. Reder, M. McClure and A. Jolley (eds) *Family matters: Interfaces between child and adult mental health*, London: Routledge, pp 3-20.

Reder, P., McClure, M. and Jolley, A. (2000c) 'Addressing the interfaces', in P. Reder, M. McClure and A. Jolley (eds) *Family matters: Interfaces between child and adult mental health*, London: Routledge, pp 318-30.

Regier, D., Boyd, J., Burke, J. et al (1988) 'One month of prevalence of mental disorders in the USA', *Archives of General Psychiatry*, vol 45, pp 977-86.

Richardson, G., Chiswick, D. and Nutting, I. (1997) *Report of the inquiry into the treatment and care of Darren Carr*, Reading: Berkshire Health Authority.

Rickwood, D.J. and Braithwaite, V.A. (1994) 'Social psychological factors affecting help seeking for emotional problems', *Social Science and Medicine*, vol 39, no 4, pp 338-46.

Ritchie, J.H., Dick, D. and Lingham, R. (1994) *The report of the inquiry into the care and treatment of Christopher Clunis*, London: HMSO.

Rogers, A. and Pilgrim, D. (2001) *Mental health policy in Britain* (2nd edn), Basingstoke: Palgrave.

Rouse, S. (2002) 'Protecting children: the role of the health visitor', in K. Wilson and A. James (eds) *The child protection handbook* (2nd edn), London: Ballière Tindall, pp 305-18.

Royal College of Psychiatrists (2002) *Patients as parents: Addressing the needs, including the safety, of children whose parents have mental illness* (Council Report CR105), London: Royal College of Psychiatrists.

Rutter, M. (1985) 'Resilience in the face of adversity: protective factors and resilience to psychiatric disorder', *British Journal of Psychiatry*, vol 147, pp 598-611.

Rutter, M. (1990) 'Commentary: some focus and process considerations regarding effects of parental depression on children', *Developmental Psychology*, vol 26, pp 60-7.

Ryan, M. (2000) *Working with fathers*, Oxford: Radcliffe Medical Press.

Sainsbury Centre for Mental Health (1997) *Pulling together: The future roles and training of mental health staff*, London: The Sainsbury Centre for Mental Health.

Samson, C. (1995) 'The fracturing of medical dominance in British psychiatry', *Sociology of Health and Illness*, vol 172, no 2, pp 245-69.

Sands, R. (1995) 'The parenting experience of low-income single women with serious mental disorders', *Families in Society: The Journal of Contemporary Human Services*, pp 86-96.

Sayce, L. (2000) *From psychiatric patient to citizen: Overcoming discrimination and sexual exclusion*, Basingstoke: Macmillan.

Schneider, J. (1993) 'Care programming in mental health: assimilation and adaption', *British Journal of Social Work*, vol 23, no 4, pp 383-403.

Scott, D.W. and Russell, L. (2001) 'Contracting: the experience of service delivery
in M. Harris and C. Rochester (eds) *Voluntary organisations and social*

Sheppard, M. (1990) *Mental health: The role of the approved social worker*, Sheffield: Joint Unit for Social Services Research, Sheffield University.

Sheppard, M. (1995) *Care management and the new social work*, London: Whiting and Birch.

Sheppard, M. (1997) 'Double jeopardy: the link between child abuse and maternal depression in child and family social work', *Child and Family Social Work*, vol 2, no 2, pp 91-107.

Sheppard, M. (2002) 'Depressed mothers' experience of partnership in child and family care', *British Journal of Social Work*, vol 32, pp 93-112.

Sheppard, M. with Kelly, N. (2001) *Social work practice with depressed mothers in child and family care,* London: The Stationery Office.

Showalter, E. (1987) *The female malady: Women, madness and English culture*, London: Virago.

Sidebotham, P. (2001) 'An ecological approach to child abuse: a creative use of scientific models in research and practice', *Child Abuse Review*, vol 10, no 2, pp 97-112.

Social Services Committee (1984) *Children in care* (HC 360), London: HMSO.

SSI (Social Services Inspectorate) (1996) *Social services departments and the care programme approach: An inspection*, London: DoH.

SSI (1999) *Still building bridges: The report of a national inspection of arrangements for the integration of care programme approach with care management*, London: DoH.

SSI (2002) *Delivering quality children's services: Inspection of children's services*, London: DoH.

Stanley, N. and Manthorpe, J. (1997) 'Risk assessment: developing training for professionals in mental health work', *Social Work and Social Sciences Review*, vol 7, no 1, pp 26-38.

Stanley, N. and Manthorpe, J. (2001) 'Reading mental health inquiries: messages for social work', *Journal of Social Work*, vol 1, no 1, pp 77-99.

Stanley, N. and Manthorpe, J. (eds) (2004: forthcoming) *The age of inquiries: Learning and blaming in health and social care*, London: Routledge.

Stanley, N., Manthorpe, J., Bradley, G. and Alaszewski, A. (1998) 'Researching community care assessments: a pluralistic approach', in J. Cheetham and M.A.F. Kazi (eds) *The working of social work*, London: Jessica Kingsley, pp 69-84.

Stanley, N. and Penhale, B. (1999) 'The mental health problems of mothers experiencing the child protection system: identifying needs and appropriate responses', *Child Abuse Review*, vol 8, no 1, pp 34-45.

Statham, J., Dillon, J. and Moss, P. (2001) *Placed and paid for – Supporting families through sponsored day care*, London: The Stationery Office.

Stevenson, O. (1989) 'Multi-disciplinary work in child protection', in O. Stevenson (ed) *Child abuse: Public policy and professional practice*, Hemel Hempstead: Harvester Wheatsheaf, pp 173-203.

Stevenson, O. (1999) 'Children in need and abused: interprofessional and interagency responses', in O. Stevenson (ed) *Child welfare in the UK 1948-1998*, Oxford: Blackwell Science Ltd, pp 100-20.

Strauss, A. and Corbin, J. (1990) *Basics of qualitative research: Grounded theory, procedures and techniques*, London: Sage Publications.

Stroud, J. and Pritchard, C. (2001) 'Child homicide, psychiatric disorder and dangerousness: a review and an empirical approach', *British Journal of Social Work*, vol 31, no 2, pp 249-70.

Targosz, S., Bebbington, P., Lewis, G., Brugha, T., Jenkins, R. Farrell, M. and Meltzer, H. (2003) 'Lone mothers, social exclusion and depression', *Psychological Medicine*, no 33, pp 715-22.

Thoburn, J., Lewis, A. and Shemmings, D. (1995) *Paternalism or partnership? Family involvement in the child protection process*, London: HMSO.

Trowell, J. (2001) 'Confidentiality and child protection', in C. Cordess (ed) *Confidentiality and mental health*, London: Jessica Kingsley, pp 85-94.

Tunstill, J. (1997) 'Implementing the family support clauses of the 1989 Children Act: legislative, professional and organisational obstacles', in N. Parton (ed) *Child protection and family support: Tensions, contradictions and possibilities*, London: Routledge, pp 39-58.

Tunstill, J. and Aldgate, J. (2000) *Services for children in need: From policy to practice*, London: The Stationery Office.

Tye, C. and Precey, G. (1999) 'Building bridges: the interface between adult mental health and child protection', *Child Abuse Review*, vol 8, pp 164-71.

~~[illegible]~~ (2003) 'What works in primary care?', in A. Cohen (ed)

Weir, A. (1999) 'An introduction to the issues: a new holistic approach outlined', in A. Weir and A. Douglas (eds) *Child protection and adult mental health*, Oxford: Butterworth Heinemann.

Weir, A. and Douglas, A. (eds) (1999) *Child protection and adult mental health*, Oxford: Butterworth Heinemann, pp 1-9.

Weir, B.W., Lynch, E., Hodes, D.H. and Goodhart, C.L. (1997) 'The role of the general practitioner in child protection and family support: a collaborative training model', *Child Abuse Review*, vol 6, pp 65-9.

Wellard, S. (2003) 'Women only', *Community Care*, 10-16 April, no 1467, pp 34-5.

Wilczynski, A. (1997) *Child homicide*, London: Greenwich Medical Media.

Williams, P., Tarnopolsky, A., Hand, D. and Shepherd, M. (1986) 'Minor psychiatric morbidity and general practice consultations: the West London Survey', *Psychological Medicine Monograph Supplement*, vol 9.

Wilson, C. (2002) *Breaking down the barriers,* London: Youth Access.

Winchester, R. (2003) 'Take a break', *Community Care*, 27 March-2 April, no 1465, pp 36-7.

Wood, J., Ashman, M., Davies, C., Lloyd, H. and Lockett, K. (1996) *Report of the inquiry into the care of Anthony Smith*, Derby: Southern Derbyshire Health Authority/Derbyshire County Council.

Woodcock, J. (2003) 'The social work assessment of parenting: an exploration', *British Journal of Social Work*, vol 33, no 1, pp 87-106.

Woodley, L., Dixon, K., Lindow, V., Oyebode, O., Sandford, T. and Simblet, S. (1995) *The Woodley Team Report*, London: East London and City Health Authority and Newham Council.

YoungMinds (2002) *Mental health services for adolescents and young adults*, London: YoungMinds.

Index

Page references for tables are in *italics*.

Also available from The Policy Press

Working together or pulling apart?

The National Health Service and child protection networks

Carol Lupton, Social Services Research and

Children caring for parents with mental illness

Perspectives of young carers, parents and professionals

Jo Aldridge and **Saul Becker**, Centre for Child and Family Research, Loughborough University

Paperback £19.99 ISBN 1 86134 399 X
234 x 156mm 224 pages March 2003

Parenting and disability

Disabled parents' experiences of raising children

Richard Olsen, Department of Epidemiology, Nuffield Community Care Studies Unit, University of Leicester and **Harriet Clarke**, Institute of Applied Social Studies, University of Birmingham

Paperback £18.99 ISBN 1 86134 364 7
234 x 156mm 208 pages April 2003

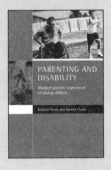

→

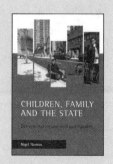